STUDIES IN ENGLISH LITERATURE

Volume XLV

EROS AND THE ROMANTICS

SEXUAL LOVE AS A THEME IN COLERIDGE, SHELLEY AND KEATS

by

GERALD ENSCOE

Franklin and Marshall College
Lancaster

1967

MOUTON

THE HAGUE · PARIS

LIBRARY OF CONGRESS CATALOG CARD NUMBER: 67-30548

Printed in The Netherlands by Mouton & Co., Printers, The Hague

To Edward E. Bostetter in grateful
acknowledgment of his invaluable
assistance.

TABLE OF CONTENTS

I

DYNAMIC ORGANICISM AND ROMANTIC FRAMES OF REFERENCE

In the last three chapters of *The Great Chain of Being*, Lovejoy describes the breakup toward the end of the eighteenth century of the magnificent and highly ordered metaphysical structure which had dominated European thought since the time of Plato and Aristotle. It is hardly necessary here to summarize Lovejoy's concept of the Great Chain; but reduced to its bare essentials, it is a concept which sees creation as a single act in which everything possible or necessary was either present or somehow implicit from the beginning. Furthermore, all possibilities of existence were arranged in an ordered hierarchy from the deity down to non-existence, each segment of creation having its own place in the highly organized scheme of things.

This principle of plenitude, upon which the whole structure of the Great Chain was based, was essentially static and mechanistic. It was, in fact,

inconsistent with any belief in progress, or indeed, in any sort of significant change in the universe as a whole. The Chain of Being, in so far as its continuity and completeness were affirmed on the customary grounds, was a perfect example of an absolutely rigid and static scheme of things.[1]

The metaphor which best expresses the rigidity of this system is that of a machine, or as some eighteenth century metaphysicians would have put it, a watch: a perfectly running watch in which every existing part is meant to contribute to the harmonious work-

---

[1] Arthur O. Lovejoy, *The Great Chain of Being* (Cambridge, Harvard University Press, 1936), p. 242.

ing of the whole. If imperfections seem to exist, they are illusions, for which the limitations of human understanding are responsible. Evil can be defined as a failure to know one's place in the system, or an attempt to function in some role in the system for which one is not created. Man's fall from grace is a direct result of his failure to keep in tune with the perfect harmony of the universe. In short, the universe was a God-centered one, with man but one element in the totality, albeit a special and important element.

But, as Lovejoy shows, this highly ordered concept of being had begun to disintegrate by the eighteenth century as the internal inconsistencies of the system began to become more glaring. For centuries it had been assumed that

> Reason – usually conceived as summed up in the knowledge of a few simple and self-evident truths – is the same in all men and equally possessed by all; and therefore that universal and equal intelligibility, universal acceptability, and even universal familiarity, to all normal members of the human species, regardless of difference of time, place, race, and individual propensities and endowments, constitute the decisive criterion of validity or of worth in all matters of vital human concernment.[2]

The intellectual and metaphysical basis of the literary phenomena "Romanticism" was the gradual emergence of a belief in exactly the contrary:

> There have, in the entire history of thought, been few changes in standards of value more profound and more momentous than that which took place when ... it came to be believed not only that in many, or in all, phases of human life there are diverse excellences, but that diversity itself is of the essence of excellence. ... And this assumption though assuredly not the only important, is the one *common*, factor in a number of otherwise diverse tendencies which ... have been termed "Romantic".[3]

The reasons for the disintegration of the traditional concept do not really concern us here; we are concerned only with the evidence that such a disintegration took place and with the new system of thought that replaced it. For by the time of the great English

---

[2] *Ibid.*, pp. 288-289.
[3] *Ibid.*, p. 293.

Romantic poets, a new cosmic orientation with an accompanying moral reorientation is observable in most of the assumptions upon which their poetry is based.

Morse Peckham has called this new conception of the cosmos that of a *dynamic organism* as opposed to the older concept of a static mechanism. Mr. Peckham's discussion, based upon Love-joy's observations, is a clarifying one and should be presented in some detail.

Let us begin with the new metaphor. The new metaphor is not a machine; it is an organism. It is a tree, for example; and a tree is a good example, for a study of nineteenth century literature reveals the continual recurrence of that image. Hence the new thought is organicism. Now the first quality of an organism is that it is not something made, it is something being made or growing. We have a philosophy of becoming, not a philosophy of being. Furthermore, the relation of its component parts is not that of the parts of a machine which have been made separately, i.e., separate entities in the mind of the deity, but the relation of leaves to stem to trunk to root to earth. Entities are an organic part of that which produced them. The existence of each part is made possible only by the existence of every other part. Relationships, not entities, are the object of contemplation and study.[4]

Thus, Mr. Peckham goes on, the universe "is not something made, a perfect machine; it grows" (p. 10). And if the universe, by its very nature is growing, it is consequently changing, for growth implies change. Therefore, "change becomes a positive value, not a negative value; change is not man's punishment, it is his opportunity" (p. 10). The whole concept of perfection also undergoes a rather radical change. If the universe is growing, it cannot be growing away from perfection, for anything that grows or changes qualitatively cannot be perfect and perhaps will never be perfect. "Perfection ceases to be a positive value. Imperfection becomes a positive value" (p. 11). With change, novelty and newness are constantly intruding upon the world, and with each new intrusion, "the fundamental character of the universe itself changes. We have a universe of emergents" (p. 11). Thus, instead of a universe with

---

[4] Morse Peckham, "Toward a Theory of Romanticism", *PMLA*, LXVI (March, 1951), p. 10.

established and pre-existent patterns, we have a universe in which the pattern for each new emergent is established by the nature of the emergent itself. Instead of an ordered hierarchy of values, we have values establishing themselves as they emerge from nothingness.

In its radical form, dynamic organicism results in the idea that the history of the universe is the history of God creating himself. Evil is at least accounted for, since the history of the universe – God being imperfect to begin with – is the history of God, whether transcendent or immanent, ridding himself, by the evolutionary process, of evil. . . . In a metaphysical nutshell, the older philosophy grounded itself on the principle that nothing can come from nothing. The newer philosophy grounded itself on the principle that something can come from nothing, that an excess can come from a deficiency, that nothing succeeds like excess. (p. 11.)

Mr. Peckham is aware that this new cosmic conception is far from a conscious, elaborately worked out system, accepted without question by the best minds among the Romantics. All we can say is that in trying to understand the nature of the change in thought which seems to have taken place in the late eighteenth century and early nineteenth century, that change which in all its manifold forms has been labeled "Romanticism", the idea of the dynamic organism makes many of the somewhat confusing aspects of Romantic thought more comprehensible. And without necessarily accepting this idea in all of its details, as elaborated upon by Mr. Peckham, we can nonetheless use it as a convenient metaphor for clearing up some of the confusion.

Certainly one of the barriers in the way of understanding much of Romantic poetry has been the failure to see the vastly different metaphysical frame of reference of this poetry which separates it from the poetry of the past, particularly that of the sixteenth and seventeenth centuries. Such poetry, according to R. A. Foakes, has based most of its important references on the concept of an external order in the universe.

Actions, ideas, relationships of characters, were inevitably posed against an ordering of the world, a religious ordering in as much as it led up to God, which established their value and distinguished clearly between right and wrong, good and bad. Any story tended to acquire symbolic or allegorical significance in the light of this concept, and could be used to embody profound ideas and feelings about man and the world, could become topical in the largest sense. It is significant that most literature prior to the middle of the eighteenth century tells a story, or at least says what it has to say in terms of a world, events, and people outside the author himself.[5]

The Romantic poets, however, lived in and wrote for a society which could no longer be described meaningfully in terms of this concept of cosmic, or for that matter, moral order. The hierarchy of meaningful experience, in which the highest values were those which led up to God, had disintegrated under various social and philosophical pressures; and as Foakes puts it, the disparity between the real world and the ideal order had become so manifest that it was no longer possible to accept this ideal order, even as a myth.

The growth of the middle class, of industry and trade, the decline of the monarchy and the aristocracy as representatives of power, and the approach of democracy were capped, for the early Romantic poets at any rate, by the French Revolution, Godwin's notions of a perfect society as a blithe anarchy, and pantisocracy. The old concept of an external order in the universe had gone, and was replaced by various ideas, which, like Godwin's theory, postulated the possibility of the self-fulfillment of the individual man as an ideal. (p. 41.)

Thus when the Romantic poets dealt with the relationships of man in the world, it was a world vastly different from the world of their predecessors. It was a world apprehensible primarily through the senses, a world centered around man and the individual. The things of this world did not necessarily reflect the glory of God: instead they were the means by which God could, if he existed, be made comprehensible. It was not God becoming flesh that was miraculous; it was the flesh revealing God, or hinting at his true nature, that contained the miracle. The values of this world by which human action could be judged were not necessarily good because of their proximity to a God external to man. Byron's *Cain* denounces the traditional concept of the deity: God has committed

---

[5]   R. A. Foakes, *The Romantic Assertion* (New Haven, Yale University Press, 1958), p. 39.

a cosmic sin by refusing to allow man the dignity of being fully human. Shelley's *Prometheus Unbound* attacks the traditional God and glorifies the figure of Prometheus, the symbol of a suffering humanity.

The collapse of a frame of reference outside of man and the natural world, led these poets to search for values and principles of action either within themselves or in the natural world. These values are not pre-ordained but emergent; and as they emerge, as they are discovered, they reveal new possibilities for moral evaluation.

Wordsworth, for example, discovers one of the supreme virtues to be a natural, unforced, spontaneous approach to living. In the highly moralistic *Ode to Duty*, although a somewhat traditional notion of duty is deified, this concept is finally defined as a kind of prescription to cure the spirit when the natural and spontaneous fails:

> There are who ask not if thine eye
> Be on them; who, in love and truth,
> Where no misgiving is, rely
> Upon the genial sense of youth:
> Glad hearts! without reproach or blot
> Who do thy work and know it not. (p. 385.)[6]

The truly blessed are those who can function without the "stern daughter's" eye upon them. These are the "glad hearts" who can operate under the benign influence of love and truth with no need of the stern "lawgiver". A sense of duty may be necessary, and the poet prays for it to descend and assist him; but, it is equally stressed, nothing about it is absolute. True serenity will be ours when we can work through the beneficent influence of love:

> Serene will be our days and bright
> And happy will our nature be
> When love is an unerring light
> And joy its own security.

[6] Citations from Wordsworth in my text are to *The Poetical Works of Wordsworth*, ed. Thomas Hutchinson, revised by Ernest De Selincourt (London, Oxford University Press, 1960).

Stallknecht has called this central concept in Wordsworth's poetry the "ethics of freedom",[7] an ethics in which the highest ideals are freedom and autonomous selfhood. Not by conscious dedication to a rigid, intellectualized moral order is man's life made meaningful, but by an essentially passive response to experience. Wordsworth, according to Mr. Stallknecht, tells us that

> our life in these modern times . . . is overintellectualized in its orientation and too practical in its interests. Hence our view of the world is falsified and our scale of values distorted. These errors cannot be corrected merely by taking thought, but by fashioning a new way of life to replace that mode of living of which our dismal philosophies are symptoms.[8]

Significant experience for Wordsworth is the result of a wise passiveness rather than dedicated activity. Man must seek a form of mystic awareness,

> . . . a sense sublime
> Of something far more deeply interfused
> Whose dwelling is the light of setting suns,
> And the round ocean and the living air
> And the blue sky, and in the mind of man.
> (*Tintern Abbey*, p. 163)

And this awareness comes as a spontaneous and genial influence from the natural world.

In the well-known *Expostulation and Reply*, this point is developed in dramatic terms and given philosophical justification. The young scholar is chastised by his tutor for dreaming, for his passivity. He should be concentrating upon his books:

> Why, William, sit you thus alone,
> And dream your life away?
> Where are your books – that light bequeathed
> To Beings else forlorn and blind!
> Up! up! and drink the spirit breathed
> From dead men to their kind. (p. 377.)

---

[7] Newton P. Stallknecht, "Wordsworth and the Quality of Man", *The Major English Romantic Poets* (Carbondale, Southern Illinois University Press, 1957), p. 71.
[8] Newton P. Stallknecht, *Strange Seas of Thought* (Bloomington, Indiana University Press, 1958), p. 3.

This admonition to forget natural inclinations in favor of useful activity is, of course, only a blank charge: a foil against which to measure the words of the idle scholar. "From dead men to their kind" ironically defines the activities demanded of the student, suggesting that following the master's advice leads to death.

The master continues his exhortation, describing an overly intellectualized, dutiful approach to life:

> You look round on your Mother Earth,
> As if she for no purpose bore you;
> As if you were her first-born birth,
> And none had lived before you!

Life, according to the Master, has a plan, a purpose, an organization. We must make, consciously and by deliberate effort, the most of our energies. Without this knowledge, this tradition, this "spirit breathed from dead men to their kind", we are nothing.

In the "Reply", the young scholar justifies his passivity, denying that a conscious, rational, and deliberate search for knowledge is the only way to learn:

> The eye – it cannot chose but see;
> We cannot bid the ear be still;
> Our bodies feel, where'er they be,
> Against or with our will.

We learn by existing in harmonious relationship with the earth; the processes of sense, seeing, hearing, feeling, are a means of learning. And this sensuous apprehension of experience is opposed to the educational organization of the master.

Dreaming, we learn, has a value: the powers of the natural world impress our minds by simple, unconscious, natural processes:

> . . . I deem that there are Powers
> Which of themselves our minds impress;
> That we can feed this mind of ours
> In a wise passiveness.
>
> Think you, 'mid all this mighty sum
> Of things for ever speaking,
> That nothing of itself will come,
> But we must still be seeking?

In what seems a deliberate reversal of values, one of the seven deadly sins, *sloth*, is elevated into a virtue: a virtue to be contrasted with and evaluated against industry and intellectual effort. The dedicated life is devalued; simple, sensuous perception of the world, spontaneous experience, are more important than the life of dedication.

The glorification of nature and natural spontaneity is not, of course, in itself a completely new theme; a large group of "pre-Romantic" nature poets, writing in the late eighteenth century, had begun to celebrate nature in their poetry a generation before Wordsworth and the other Romantics. Joseph Warton sings the praises of the countryside as early as 1744, calling upon the "green-robed Dryads" of the country to lead him from "gardens decked with art's vain pomps". Nature, to Warton, is the source of imagination and creativity; the ancient bards were "sweet Nature's friends", and the muse of the country has taught them the "moral strains ... to mend mankind".[9] And Mark Akenside's *The Pleasures of Imagination*, is subtitled, *The Aesthetic and Moral Influence of Nature.*[10] Akenside philosophically declares, like Wordsworth's young scholar, that dedication and obedience are not the means to produce great art:

> ... for fruitless is the attempt
> By dull obedience and by creeping toil
> Obscure, to conquer the severe ascent
> Of high Parnassus. (I, 34-37.)

The true poet must seek his inspiration from Nature:

> Nature's kindling breath
> Must fire the chosen genius; Nature's hand
> Must string his nerves, and imp his eagle-wings,
> Impatient of the painful steep, to soar
> High as the summit, there to breathe at large
> Ethereal air, with bards and sages old,
> Immortal sons of praise. (I, 37-43.)

[9] "The Enthusiast: Or The Lover of Nature", in *English Poems from Dryden to Blake*, ed. James W. Tupper (New York, Prentice-Hall, 1933), p. 492.
[10] Citations from Akenside's poem are to *The Works of the English Poets*, ed. Alexander Chalmers, XIV (1810), pp. 60-80.

But although similarities are to be found here to Wordsworth's glorification of the natural world, a significant difference is also discernible. Akenside is still committed to a traditional cosmic structure and glorifies Nature because Nature leads us upward to an understanding of God, because it is a sign of his omnipotent goodness:

> God alone . . .
> Imprints the secret bias of the soul.
> He, mighty parent! wise and just in all,
> Free as the vital breeze, or light of heaven,
> Reveals the charms of Nature. (III, 522-26.)

God is still external, elevated above the natural world; nature has been created for man, particularly the poet, to draw upon for creative inspiration; it is a stepping stone to God:

> Thus the men
> Whom Nature's work can charm, with God himself
> Hold converse; grow familiar day by day
> With his conceptions; act upon his plan;
> And form to his, the relish of their souls. (III, 629-633.)

However, to Wordsworth, God is not above Nature, an external creator and manipulator. Nature itself is the source of knowledge, inspiration, and perhaps morality. For in the famous section in Book I of *The Prelude*, in which the narrator describes a boat-stealing incident from his childhood, the mountain itself, "a huge peak, black and huge,/ As if with voluntary power instinct" (I, 378-379.), rises up into the sky to chastize the young thief. Although the child tries to escape the awful presence of the "grim shape", it seemed to follow him like a living thing.

> I struck and struck again
> And growing still in stature the grim shape
> Towered up between me and the stars, and still
> For so it seemed, with purpose of its own
> And measured motion like a living thing,
> Strode after me. (I, 380-85.)

Here, in the shapes of nature, is the source of moral virtue. We need look no further than the things of the world for ethical and moral illumination.

Even mystic awareness, traditionally associated with reaching a oneness with God, is defined in *Tintern Abbey* as reaching a oneness with nature. The shapes of nature, the "beauteous forms" of the natural world, are the means not to reaching God, but to establishing communion with the earth itself, a mystic and spiritual communion. To these beauteous forms the narrator owes a sublime gift:

> . . . that blessed mood
> In which the burthen of the mystery,
> In which the heavy and the weary weight
> Of all this unintelligible world,
> Is lightened: – that serene and blessed mood,
> In which the affections gently lead us on, –
> Until, the breath of this corporeal frame
> And even the motion of our human blood
> Almost suspended, we are laid asleep
> In body, and become a living soul:
> While with an eye made quiet by the power
> Of harmony, and the deep power of joy,
> We see into the life of things.

God is not in his heaven; if he exists he exists in the intelligible world, in things. This naturalizing of the deity forms the base for a rejection of the traditional system with a structure external to man and the world.

Perhaps the Romantic position is most clearly illustrated by comparing Wordsworth's celebration of the natural world with a similar celebration by a more traditional poet, one whose frame of reference is the traditional cosmic order. For in the "pre-Romantics" we can see the stirrings which ultimately lead to the Romantic position, even though they have not yet rejected, even unconsciously, the static concept of cosmic order. But in such a poem as Andrew Marvell's *The Garden*, which has many similarities to *Expostulation and Reply*, in theme and subject matter, the contrasting attitudes toward nature and the natural world are striking.

The Garden makes a statement similar in many ways to the statement of the Wordsworth poem concerning the natural world:

>Society is all but rude
>To this delicious Solitude.

And the question Marvell raises is also similar to Wordsworth's:

>How vainly men themselves amaze
>To win the Palm, the Oke, or Bayes
>
>.   .   .
>
>While all Flow'rs and all Trees do close
>To weave the Garlands of respose.

But Marvell creates, as Wordsworth does not, a metaphorical transition from this earthly garden to the symbolic garden of Eden. By bringing in the metaphor of Paradise, the natural garden in which the poet now reposes becomes a retreat, an escape back, away from a corrupted world to a world of innocence. The soul escapes into the trees, similarly to the soul moving out into the landscape in Tintern Abbey. But the mystic awareness of Marvell is achieved by joining the earthly state to a previously described heavenly one. By losing himself in the garden, in the natural world, Marvell's narrator momentarily achieves release from the corrupt world of man, and paradoxically, from the corrupt world of nature as well.

The traditional order is strongly implied: man has fallen from innocence, from Paradise. The present world is corrupt, but corrupt because of the corresponding corruption of man. This corrupt world of nature is placed in implied juxtaposition with the ideal world which in the narrator's view has an actual existence on some other plane of experience, removed from the mortal world.

But *Expostulation and Reply* makes no statement about the corruption of nature itself. Men may be corrupt if they divorce themselves from the natural world, or fail to heed the moral lessons Nature tries to implant in us; but Nature is not a retreat from corruption, a momentary escape. Wordsworth's dreamer is not escaping; he is becoming submerged into the natural world. His paradoxically "passive" activity has value – the "wise passiveness" leads to moral awareness, different from the traditional, even opposite from it in some respects, but nonetheless based upon implied ethical principles. The dreamer on the "old grey stone" may eventually understand and grasp these principles, much as the youth in *The Prelude* discovers a natural morality among the "things" of nature.

Marvell's dreamer escapes, temporarily, from the world – a world tainted, evil, and corrupt. Nature teaches us nothing in itself; the experience with Nature is not progressive, leading us to new awareness. It is a means by which the mind may withdraw "into its happiness", a means to gain a momentary vision of the ideal garden which man's corporeal body may no longer inhabit.

It is the emphasis upon the things of this world as the source of moral law and spiritual enlightenment that marks Wordsworth off from both his pre-Romantic predecessors as well as the traditional poets. And of course it is this emphasis that separates the Romantic poets as a body from the past.

The poets of the Renaissance might have focused their attention on human experience, examining human relationships rather than man's relationship with God. But it was tacitly understood that although the plane of man's activity was important now, other planes existed external to man's world. The Gods might seem hostile at times ("We are to the Gods like flies to wanton boys, they kill us for their sport."); but they exist on another level, in another sphere, directing, controlling, watching, creating, and destroying. Whatever activity man participates in, it is in the context of and gains its significance from reference to, a God-centered cosmic and moral order.

The Romantic Gods, however, are no longer external *beings* but external *symbols*: symbols of internal states. The Gods are humanized, and the cosmic battle between good and evil becomes a purely human struggle between opposing psychic forces. This view of the Gods can be best seen in some of the major Romantic poetry dealing with the subject of sexual love. Perhaps no single theme could better illustrate this shift in cosmic and moral orientation, for certainly erotic passion is one of the internal forces the traditional Christian ethos has attempted to control, to legislate, and to denigrate in the moral scale. The plight of the poor mortal who allows himself to be lowered on the divine scale by giving in to sexual temptation has been the subject of countless poems in

European literature. And at the center of the conflict, at least in the traditional treatment of the subject, is the assumption that the passions, based upon a sensual response to life, lead us away from God toward the bestial orders of experience. The world, the flesh, and the devil keep us from salvation, if we give in to the admittedly attractive appeal of this unholy trinity.

But the Romantic ethos is based upon acceptance of and even dedication to these natural forces, and we shall notice in the following chapters a dramatic shift away from moral evaluation based upon an abstract, intellectual system. As I hope to demonstrate, the three Romantic poets who deal in any detail with the subject of erotic passion, see such passion not as an inherently evil force pulling man away from salvation, but as a force which has the possibility of leading him to psychic regeneration.

Coleridge, in *Kubla Khan* and *Christabel*, is highly ambivalent in his attitudes toward the erotic, but he seems to realize, sometimes with real horror, that sexual forces in the human psyche must inevitably destroy the intellectualized and ordered dreams of the abstract mind. Shelley in both *Alastor* and *Epipsychidion,* makes sexual love the basis for reaching an idealized state of internal harmony. And Keats, in four major poems, deifies erotic passion, making its symbols objects of worship, replacing the old god of reason. To Keats the sexual relationship may be the means by which man may gain whatever divinity it is his to possess, even though a constant struggle exists between the forces of love and the forces of reason, the outcome of which is doubtful. The reasoned and rational world must, it seems, destroy the erotic dream, almost in self-defense.

Throughout the work of these poets, erotic sensibility is undergoing a process of re-evaluation. Less and less are the passions seen as the allies of corruption, capable of reducing man to a level of bestiality. They are beginning to see the integral nature of all the forces operative in the human psyche, and in their works erotic passion is beginning to emerge, not as an essentially evil force pulling man from virtue and from God, but a force that man must accept and trust as a part of his total nature: a force which through a freedom of expression beyond the limits of an externally imposed morality may free man from his centuries-old psycho-machia.

It may be true that none of the poets we shall subsequently examine are entirely free from the internal conflict generated by the war between sense and reason; but in varying ways each demonstrates considerable psychological awareness in sexual matters which can only be understood totally, I think, within the context of an earth-centered, man-centered, cosmic view. The truth is no longer fixed and absolute within an ordered frame of reference. The metaphor of the dynamic organicism, postulating as it does, a growing toward a truth not yet realized, best describes this idea. And in order to grow, the Romantic poets had first to liberate themselves, as well as the human spirit, from what had proven to be the confinement of traditional Christian ethics.

As Wordsworth tried to redeem nature and the external world from the labels "corrupt" and "fallen", Shelley, Keats, and Coleridge examine the traditional association of the flesh with the devil, hoping, perhaps, to redeem the flesh from this guilt by association. This separation of the devil from his traditional allies, if it does not destroy him, at least gives hope of bringing about some form of "peace with honor". We see in the following chapters the beginnings in these poets of modern psychological awareness, an awareness that has revolutionized our approaches to moral and ethical evaluation of man's sexual experience.

II

COLERIDGE'S *KUBLA KHAN* AND *CHRISTABEL:* STUDIES IN EROTIC AMBIGUITY

Stephen Potter, in an illuminating psycho-biographical study of Coleridge, has argued cogently the case for a rather schizophrenic Coleridge, a composite of two widely contrasting types. On the one hand is the public image representing the conscious, moral, fixed ego presented to the world and to himself. On the other hand is the "continuously evolving, experiencing, truly living person".[1] In reading Coleridge, we must bear in mind always this composite picture and be careful to distinguish between the public "character" and the private "personality", or what Blake would probably call the "Identity" as opposed to the "self". Mr. Potter has, I think, called our attention to an important consideration which the serious student of Coleridge's poetry must constantly keep in mind: a characteristic ambivalence with which Coleridge often approaches certain themes, particularly themes with complex moral and philosophical overtones.

I wish to consider this ambivalence not as a means of describing in any biographical sense the "real" Coleridge, but as a term to describe an effective use of symbol and metaphor as conductors of poetic meaning. I think it has been abundantly illustrated by now, both through perceptive readings of his poems and detailed examinations of his criticism, that the animadversions of such critics as E. E. Stoll, and Miss Elizabeth Schneider notwithstanding,[2] Coleridge was quite capable of loading every rift of

[1] Stephen Potter, *Coleridge and S. T. C.* (Toronto, Thomas Nelson and Sons, 1935), p. 16.
[2] E. E. Stoll, "Symbolism in Coleridge", *PMLA*, LXIII (1948), pp. 214-233; Elizabeth Schneider, *Coleridge, Opium and "Kubla Khan"* (Chicago, University of Chicago Press, 1953).

his best poetry with symbolic ore. And as Marshall Suther has effectively demonstrated, Coleridge can be seen as the great originator of many of the so-called "modern" concepts of symbolic meaning.[3]

Robert Penn Warren's reading of *The Ancient Mariner*,[4] for example, cannot be discredited upon the grounds that Coleridge lacked any such specific, conscious purpose, or that the symbolic overtones connected with the murder of the albatross are "modern notions", of which Coleridge would have no understanding. Mr. Warren's analysis is substantiated by the imagery and structure of the poem; and even if the shade of Coleridge could be summoned to deny any such conscious intention, the poem itself would contradict the public statement. (I suspect that even the shade of Coleridge would be composed more of character than of personality.) In fact, if we are not prepared to read *The Ancient Mariner* as a complex and somewhat ambivalent utterance, we must feel that Coleridge is writing for children, and not very bright children at that. The simplified moral,

> He prayeth best who loveth best
> All things both great and small
> For the dear God who loveth us
> He made and loveth all.

if allowed to stand as the poem's "meaning", is a trite and far from enlightened commentary upon man's experience in this world. And even though Mr. Potter's public "character" might have been capable of an utterance to the effect that stepping on a worm is an act to be punished by all the celestial machinery of the gods, such a statement hardly accounts for the aesthetic involvement the poem produces upon the mature reader.

The Mariner is described with considerable ambivalence. He is touched by some suggestion of the super-natural; his "glittering eye" holds the Wedding-Guest in a powerful spell, from which he

---

[3] Marshall Suther, "On the Interpretation of *Kubla Khan*", *Bucknell Review*, VII (May, 1957), pp. 1-19.
[4] Robert Penn Warren, "Poem of Pure Imagination", in *Rime of the Ancient Mariner* (New York, Reynal Publishing Company, 1946).

is unable to break away. He is like a spectre, similar to those un-
easy spirits of mythology who cannot sleep because of some crime
or sin they must expiate:

> I pass, like night, from land to land;
> I have strange power of speech; (586-87)[5]

He has some powerful mission to accomplish; the men to whom
he tells his tale of expiation and suffering are singled out from all
others, presumably to receive some kind of insight or enlightenment:

> That moment that his face I see,
> I know the man that must hear me:
> To him my tale I teach. (588-90)

When the ship touches land after the horrible pilgrimage, the
Pilot's boy goes mad at the sight of him, confusing him with the
devil himself:

> "Ha! ha!" quoth he, "full plain I see,
> The Devil knows how to row". (568-69)

Yet this creature, suggesting some relationship with the diabolical,
utters Christian truths, the Christian idea of the good life:

> "O sweeter than the marriage-feast,
> 'Tis sweeter far to me,
> To walk together to the kirk
> With a goodly company! —
>
> To walk together to the kirk,
> And all together pray,
> While each to his great Father bends,
> Old men, and babes, and loving friends,
> And youths and maidens gay! (601-09)

Surely some attempt is made here to establish a relationship,
perhaps even a partnership, between the forces of good and evil.
The Mariner, although in appearance and manner associated with
the demonic and supernatural, has a sobering effect upon the
Wedding-Guest who from his encounter goes forth

---

[5] Citations to Coleridge in my text are to *Poems of Coleridge* (London,
Oxford University Press, 1960).

> ... like one that hath been stunned,
> And is of sense forlorn:
> A sadder and a wiser man,
> He rose the morrow morn. (622-25)

Somehow that which in appearance suggests evil becomes an instrument for spreading awareness and moral enlightenment.

If this were all, the theme would not differ greatly from Milton's theme of God producing good out of evil. But Satan, as Milton demonstrates with no ambivalence or ambiguity, is to be seen as the embodiment of evil. He is not the agent of good operating in what seems to be an evil context; he is evil personified and, by his actions, defined.

But it would be absurd to insist that the Mariner is evil or Satanic. He is perhaps an agent of some supernatural power, but his mission is specifically one of enlightenment, and he himself seems conscious of this higher purpose. He tells a story of sin and expiation; and although the Wedding-Guest fears him and tries to escape from him, he must listen. He has no choice. His fear is gradually transformed, as the tale unfolds, to fascination and even pity; and this combination of fear and fascination actually produces moral change. At the conclusion of the tale he is chastened and subdued, a sadder but wiser man. Our response to the Mariner is a mixture of these same emotions; we fear him and yet gradually come to pity him. His sufferings are so out of proportion to his apparent sin that his moral homily at the end of the poem seems almost hollow – this was a terrible price to pay for such awareness. We may accept it in the context of the poem, but with considerable ambivalence. This may be the way divine providence works, but such divine providence seems sadly lacking in humanitarian principles.

Thus the key word to describe the poet's attitude toward this central character is "ambivalence". He forces his readers to suspend any straight-forward, simplified judgments concerning the Mariner, and the total effect is to present a kind of moral stasis. It is impossible to respond to the poem with any stock interpretation, and our responses tend to become as ambivalent as the poet's presentation of the Mariner in the poem. However, a simple recognition of this characteristic ambivalence is not enough to define and understand the poet's intentions. The fact that a poet looks two ways at his subject matter may just as easily indicate confusion as symbolic capability. It is equally important to see what, if any, symbolic attitude is taken toward the subject matter, what "meanings" are contained in the contradictions.

In the case of the *Ancient Mariner*, the contradictions are rather neatly resolved in that the diabolical appearance of the Mariner, his strange supernatural qualities, are means to an end – an end contained within the structure of the poem. The Mariner is strange, perhaps demonic, but no suspicion exists about his ultimate function: he is to redeem the world, at least a small part of it, by playing out his role as a wandering teller of tales. Like a poet, he tells his story and the telling of it produces change. But what he has to tell is not particularly new or startling; it has been told before. Everything in the poem does lead to the moral tagline, which is hardly a revelation. The implications of the moral are more complicated than the unsophisticated reader of the poem might suspect, but they are nonetheless implications which can be fitted into traditional, Christian-oriented morality. Coleridge's ambivalence operates here to give symbolic depth to the poem; it does not confuse or particularly shock the reader.

But in two other poems by Coleridge, *Kubla Khan* and *Christabel*, where the subject matter is in some ways far more controversial, the contradictions involved in this ambivalent attitude are far less easy to resolve. For both of these poems deal in some way with the subject of sexual freedom, or sexual liberation. And although we may be prepared to encounter an ambivalence in Coleridge's attitude toward erotic forces, a habit of mind that causes him to be both attracted and repelled by what an analysis of these forces at work within the human psyche may reveal, it is far more difficult to distinguish here between ambivalency and confusion, if indeed such a distinction exists. We may not be particularly disconcerted to discover that Coleridge's analysis of the erotic forces causes him to occasionally project these forces into his poetry as beautiful, attractive, and overwhelmingly powerful, and at the same time as terrifying and repulsive. The figure of

Geraldine, as we shall see presently, is a composite of such attitudes – she is both evil and good, beautiful and hideous, pitiful and terrifying. And this same tension produced by contrasting attitudes provides, I think, the essential core of *Kubla Khan*.

But if we are to see either poem as effective poetic constructs, we must attempt, I think, to isolate an attitude, an idea, a governing moral concern, which such ambivalence ultimately centers on. We might call it a philosophical or moral base which the various symbolic attitudes operate from and ultimately turn our attention toward. Otherwise, we are left with a conception of Coleridge as a confused, tormented, uncertain Hamlet, which may explain his limitations as a critic, but fails to account for his effectiveness as a poet. I think a close analysis of both poems will reveal such a base.

That a sexual theme exists in *Kubla Khan* has been recognized by many critics, notably Robert Graves and G. Wilson Knight – both of whom subject the poem to Freudian analysis and call our attention to the predominance of sexual imagery in the poem. Graves is convinced, for example, that the river falling into the cave has obvious sexual connotations, and that the Abyssinian maid is some unidentified female involved in the erotic phantasmagoria of Coleridge's opium dreams.[6] Knight, less biographical, calls our attention to the obvious sexual overtones in the lines describing the birth of the sacred river: the earth breathing in "thick fast pants", the fountain spouting with "half-intermitted burst", the "ceaseless turmoil" of the scene. This particular passage, combined with the image of the "woman wailing for her demon lover", expresses "the mystic glamour of sex that conditions human creation and something of its pagan evil magic; and touches the enigma of the creator-god beyond good and evil, responsible for eagle and boa-constrictor alike".[7]

But a more striking part of the poem is the tension established between order and chaos, the contrast within the garden of Kubla

---

[6] Robert Graves, *The Meaning of Dreams* (London, Adelphi Publishing Co., 1924), pp. 145-148.
[7] G. Wilson Knight, *The Starlit Dome* (London, Oxford University Press, 1941), pp. 91-92.

Khan between the sacred river and the dome of pleasure; or as Richard Fogle has stated it in a recent essay, "within the bounds of encircled garden, pleasure dome and the river are the opposites to be reconciled".[8]

The first lines of the poem present a concept of order, of an organized attempt to establish upon the disorder of the natural world a man-made construct:

> In Xanadu did Kubla Khan
> A stately pleasure-dome decree

The word "decree" connotes an act or imposition by fiat, a proclamation by the symbolic figure of reason or God or the ego or whatever authoritarian figure Kubla Khan is taken to represent. The dome is a "pleasure dome", certainly, but it is decreed, or set down upon the scene by order.

Surely Douglas Angus is mistaken in suggesting that the dome-like shape is a breast symbol,[9] even if it is true, as he suggests, that the bosom is one of Coleridge's most frequent images. There may well be, as Mr. Angus has argued, a psychological connection between the dome and Coleridge's own feelings about his mother, and at the end of the poem the poet's yearning for the lost security of the dome may represent his longing to return to his mother's breast. But without this biographical, psychoanalytical connection, which is extraneous to the language of the poem, there is little in the imagery itself to make this connection. Aside from having been "decreed" by the orders of Kubla, the dome is also "stately" which I take to mean, primarily, massive and awe-inspiring; and, if we consider the root meaning of the word, connected, as the decree itself is, with the state. It is majestic and dignified in contrast to the sacred river, which is anarchistic and free.

Immediately following this image of controlled pleasure, the poem presents a contrasting image of that which is essentially un-

---

[8] Richard H. Fogle, "The Romantic Unity of *Kubla Khan*", *College English*, XXII (November, 1960), p. 114.
[9] Douglas Angus, "The Theme of Love and Guilt in Coleridge's Three Major Poems", *JEGP*, LIX (October, 1960), pp. 664-665.

controlled and uncontrollable. The very spot upon which Kubla decides to erect his ordered pleasure dome is the spot

> Where Alph, the sacred river ran
> Through caverns measureless to man
> Down to a sunless sea.

The river running through these infinite caverns to a sunless, lightless sea is a "sacred" river, identified vaguely through its name, as Lowes points out, with one of the four rivers running out of Paradise.[10] But more important, the name suggests the Greek *alpha*, the beginning, the first, perhaps the seminal. In a later image it becomes strongly identified with the seminal stream, the creative force of life itself. Thus the first five lines of the poem establish this tension between the dome and the river, the decree and that which cannot have decrees forced upon it. The "caverns measureless to man" and the idea of the decree suggest a paradox between the thing attempted and the impossibility of success in the attempt; for if the caverns are indeed "measureless to man", then man presumably cannot measure them in order to construct his stately domes with their implied specific boundaries over them.

The description of the garden which follows elaborates this idea. The enclosed space is measured and encircled:

> So twice five miles of fertile ground
> With walls and towers were girdles round

The decree is put into effect; the area through which the sacred river runs is geometrically and logically encircled. The dome of pleasure is imposed.

Within the dome are enclosed scenes of sensuous beauty: "incense-bearing trees", "gardens bright with sinuous rills", ancient forests "enfolding sunny spots of greenery". The stately dome is pleasurable in one sense, no doubt, but it is still a restricted and encircled pleasure, "containing" the senses and ordering them. The scene of the poem suddenly shifts, however, to a place of chaos and disorder within the ordered paradise:

[10]   John Livingston Lowes, *The Road to Xanadu* (New York, Houghtor Mifflin, 1927), p. 362.

> But oh! that deep romantic chasm which slanted
> Down the green hill athwart a cedarn cover!
> A savage place! as holy and enchanted
> As e'er beneath a waning moon was haunted
> By woman wailing for her demon-lover.

The "romantic chasm" disturbs the serenity of the pleasure dome; the wild and savage scene of the woman wailing and the romantic chasm itself are "holy and enchanted". Although these two words are similar in the sense that they suggest a supernatural quality in the scene, they are not synonymous. That which is "holy" is blessed, untainted by evil or sin, sacrosanct and hallowed; "enchanted", on the other hand, suggests bewitchment and is associated with magic spells or charms. The difference between the two words is the difference between white magic and black magic.

The "romantic chasm" and the "woman wailing for her demon lover", occur in a two-fold context then: both images are in contrast to the decreed order and may ultimately lead to the destruction of this order. And such potential destruction is suggested with considerable ambiguity: the elements leading to the potential restoration of anarchy partake of the qualities of enchantment and of holiness: they are both attractive and suspect, blessed and demonic.

The poem goes on to describe in detail the violent eruption of the forces which the dome had attempted to control. It is here, in the image of the fountain leaping from the chasm, that we have the most explicit sexual imagery of the poem:

> And from this chasm, with ceaseless turmoil seething,
> As if this earth in *fast thick pants were breathing*,
> A mighty *fountain momently* was forced:
> Amid whose swift *half-intermitted burst*
> Huge fragments vaulted like rebounding hail,
> Or chaffy grain beneath the thresher's flail:
> And mid these dancing rocks at once and ever
> It flung up *momently* the *sacred river*.
>
> > (my italics)

What seems to be at least suggested here is the image of the earth itself in the throes of a sexual orgasm. Implied throughout is that the erotic impulses centered symbolically in the sacred seminal river (the demon-lover of the woman), and the orgasmic upheaval of the earth cannot be restrained by symbolic walls and towers. Within the scenes of order, the uncontrollable fountain remains, a vivid and violent reminder of disorder and chaos.

The river, after the convulsive upheaval, wanders on a chaotic, meandering course through the circumscribed five mile area, finally to drop tumultuously into the lifeless sea. It rises in confusion and energy, and, like the stream of life, ends in tumult – dispersing into eternity, in the "caverns measureless to man".

The walls and towers, the elaborate pleasure dome, have all been attempts to escape from the forces outside, from reality perhaps, as Fogle suggests:

The pleasure dome is the chosen refuge of Kubla, the mighty, the emperor whose every whim is law, who would have temptations toward *hubris*. It is the center of his retreat in his haughty withdrawal from a world unworthy of him. It is above and beyond Nature, "a miracle of rare device in which man transcends and circumvents mere natural processes".[11]

And as Kubla hears "the mingled measure/ From the fountain and the caves", he becomes acutely aware of the threat to his attempt to superimpose an external order upon the wild disorganized river and fountain. For the message he hears is clear and specific:

> . . . mid this tumult Kubla heard from far
> Ancestral voices prophesying war.

In his Jungian analysis of the poem, S. K. Heninger, Jr., suggests that this disruptive war hints at the concept of original sin with its eternal conflict between body and soul, conscious and unconscious.

Since the prophesying voices are "ancestral", they may very well belong to our first ancestors, Adam and Eve, who from their own unsettling experience proclaim the folly of seeking to know the unknowable, the futility of seeking to integrate the unconscious.[12]

---

[11] Richard Fogle, p. 114.
[12] S. K. Heninger, Jr., "A Jungian Reading of *Kubla Khan*", *Journal of Aesthetics and Art Criticism*, XVIII (March, 1960), p. 365.

But whether the cause is original sin or the neurotic explosion brought about by the ego trying to regulate too rigidly the forces of the id, the results are nonetheless potentially destructive. The plunge of the sacred river into the lifeless ocean may one day take with it the fragments of the dome. That this is a distinct possibility is suggested immediately. The dome may still exist, in spite of the violent opposition of the river and fountain; but as the narrator looks upon it, it begins to fade – he no longer sees the dome itself, only the "shadow" of it:

> The shadow of the dome of pleasure
> Floated midway on the waves.

He seems to be coming out of some kind of trance in which he is still conscious of the spectacular vision but, indefinitely, hazily, like a reflection indistinctly floating upon the waves – waves which are in movement, destroying a clear picture of even the shadow.

Suddenly the narrator shifts to the past tense:

> It *was* a miracle of rare device,
> A sunny pleasure-dome with caves of ice!

At this point the dome disappears: the vision is gone. But the speaker's final description of it perhaps indicates a new awareness of the relationship of dome to river. This relationship is conveyed in the image of the dome qualified by its opposite, the cave. And the adjectives defining each are correspondingly opposite: *sunny* for the dome, and *icy* for the caves.

Here is certainly one of the key symbols of the poem: the dome is sunny, bright, and above all *external*. The dome covers, even tries to hide, that which is under it. We see it as sunny, stately, pleasurable, and attractive when examining its surface, when on the outside looking *at* it. But the inside of a sunny dome might well be a "cave of ice", and surely the preposition *with* makes those caves of ice an integral part of the dome. The icy caves, in turn, suggest darkness, the unknown, and in opposition to the dome, the internal. The caves are those same "caverns measureless to man" which we have previously seen as the source and destination of the sacred river. As such they are intimately related in the text of the poem to the "deep romantic chasm" (another cave image) and the woman wailing.

The tone of these lines seems wistful, almost nostalgic. The narrator seems to be saying that the pleasure dome was beautiful, miraculous, and infinitely attractive – "a miracle of rare device". But there was more to the scene than the dome itself, more than the dome itself to be considered. There was that within it, in juxtaposition to it and in conflict with it, what is potentially far more powerful than the dome or its maker, Kubla Khan. And somewhat ambiguously, if we recall the "holy and enchanted" qualities of the "savage place", this force has a powerful claim upon our attention.

The tone is likewise ambiguous. If the narrator looks upon the faded dome and garden nostalgically, it does not necessarily imply an unqualified acceptance of it; nor does his reference to the caves of ice, his recognition of their existence, imply acceptance. He has seen his vision fade; he has seen the threat of the dome's destruction; and he recognizes the inevitability of the struggle. The forces threatening its destruction are both "holy" and "enchanted", however: the river is a "sacred" one. Thus the attitude of the poem toward both elements of the struggle is one of controlled ambiguity.

In the final section of the poem, the impersonal imagery in which the gardens of Xanadu have been described shifts dramatically to the personal and subjective. We have been prepared for this shift in the lines immediately preceding this, however. For the poet is coming out of his trance; in the final section he is himself again, describing another vision, the damsel with the dulcimer, but this time with the conscious self in control. What seems to be happening is that the narrator, having lost the vision of the pleasure dome, wishes to find some means by which it can be rebuilt, and he seizes upon the idea of song, music, art, or poetry, as the answer to his dilemma. The Abysinnian maid with her dulcimer, her symphony and song, strongly suggests the figure of the classical muse, the divine source of poetry. The narrator thinks:

> Could I revive within me
> Her symphony and song,

> ... with music loud and long,
> I would build that dome in air,
> That sunny dome! those caves of ice!

Having seen the original dome fade and having gained some insight into the nature of the struggle between encircling forces and measureless caverns, the poet realizes now that perhaps the vision can be recreated, "revived" through poetry. Certainly one meaning of "I would build that dome in air", is that he will, if sufficiently inspired by the muse, create the dome through art. A secondary meaning, however, arising from his new awareness, is that the dome may not exist on earth – the sacred river and the measureless caverns will not be circumscribed by domes, no matter how pleasurable and "sunny" they appear to be. The rational, the ordered, and the logical, may not be imposed arbitrarily upon the irrational, the disordered, the chaotic, without a corresponding threat of violence.

The attitude of the poem toward both areas of experience seems, then, ambivalent: the pleasure dome is sunny and pleasurable but is still an artificial escape from reality. Reality is dark and terrifying, but nonetheless holy and sacred. Only in the work of art, the symphony and song which can contain within itself both garden and river, the rational and the erotic, can there be total reconciliation. The poem containing both is art; the dome is only artificial.

The poem *Kubla Khan* is an example. Although throughout the poem the contrasting forces are seen ambivalently, both dome and river containing good and evil, the ambivalence is resolved within the total poetic structure. Without glorifying one force over the other, the poem uses the struggle and contrast between the two to make an essentially moral statement. As I have tried to show, the poem presents strong arguments against the human, perhaps we can even say humanist, tendency to restrict our erotic impulses too rigidly. It recognizes, in almost Freudian terms, the inevitable tumult in human affairs such restrictions lead to. And at the same time, the poem suggests a means of realizing our human dreams of order – through the discipline and harmony of art.

Perhaps nowhere can Coleridge's ambivalence toward the forces we have seen struggling in *Kubla Khan* be more dramatically apparent than in the widely admired and discussed, but seldom understood, *Christabel*. Not only do we have in the figure of Geraldine a fully developed personification of the erotic force suggested by the sacred river, but her seduction of Christabel is a dramatic working out of the same destruction implicit in *Kubla Khan*. Nowhere does Coleridge demonstrate in greater detail or more vividly his own ambivalent attitude toward the implications of such destruction.

That Geraldine is the embodiment of erotic impulses has been almost universally recognized in modern criticism. Arthur Nethercott's exhaustive study of the poem analyzes not only the sexual overtones associated with Geraldine, but discusses the predominantly sexual symbolism of most medieval snake-women, witches, and demons, from which he traces, through Coleridge's reading, her origins.[13]

However, Nethercott is by and large satisfied to point out these suggestions of sexual origin without comment upon their possible significance in the poem. Roy Basler, on the other hand, argues in his analysis of the poem that the sexual theme not only exists in connection with the figure of Geraldine, but furnishes the main theme of the poem.

The major action of the poem, according to Basler, involves the theme of sexual frustration:

The poem is concerned as a whole with her [Christabel's] passionate though thwarted love for the absent "betrothed knight" . . . the complication action is the preternatural, psycho-emotional influence of Geraldine, who entrances Christabel, body and soul, and enchants Christabel's father as a necessary step in effecting the continuation of Christabel's entrancement; . . . and the counteraction on a supernatural plane, which presents the spirit of Christabel's mother hovering over the distressed girl and appearing to her in two visions in order to thwart the malign influence of Geraldine.[14]

The most casual reading of the poem cannot help taking note of the overt sexuality in the bedroom scene and the obvious sexual

[13]   Arthur H. Nethercott, *The Road to Tryermaine* (Chicago, University of Chicago Press, 1939).

[14]   Roy P. Basler, *Sex, Symbolism, and Psychology in Literature* (New Brunswick, Rutgers University Press, 1948), p. 29.

enchantment of Christabel's father by Geraldine. When the poem first appeared, in fact, it was branded as obscene because of the overt sexuality of some of the passages. Nor did Coleridge ever deny the obscene label attached to the poem; he was concerned only that no reviewer or reader of the poem reproach him with charges of personal turpitude.

But granting that the poem is concerned in some way with the theme of sexual passion, the problem here is to discover what the attitude toward these forces may be. Geraldine's enchantment of the innocent Christabel is obviously a sexual one, as we shall see later; but the problem is how the reader of the poem is to respond to the enchantment. Is Geraldine, like the traditional serpent-women of mythology, a malignant being, an evil force operating against the chaste and innocent Christabel? Or is she more complicated than this, thus adding a level of complexity to our usually stock reactions to such characters?

Certainly a number of incidents occur in the early stages of the encounter to arouse our suspicions about the mysterious lady whom Christabel meets in the woods. Before they ever reach Christabel's chamber, Coleridge indicates through a series of clues that this beautiful creature is not quite the harmless abducted maiden she professes to be.

At the gate to the castle, the lady sinks to the ground as though in pain, and Christabel must carry her over the "threshold of the gate". But once inside the castle, she quickly recovers her strength. At Christabel's suggestion that they thank the Virgin for having reached the safety of the castle walls, the lady refuses, claiming that she "cannot speak for weariness". And before they reach the maiden's chamber, the mastiff bitch, who until now has never "uttered yell/ Beneath the eye of Christabel", moans angrily in her sleep as they pass. And finally, as they pass the fireplace, the dying brands of the fire burst momentarily into flame.

In short, it is fairly clear before the scene in Christabel's chamber that Geraldine is the embodiment of something mysterious, something supernatural. All four of these brief incidents reflect popular superstition that evil cannot enter a home unassisted, that demons may not offer up prayers, that dumb animals respond intuitively to the presence of evil, and that fire responds to the masters of the flames. Moreover, Geraldine's subsequent actions in the poem appear to make her the very embodiment of evil: her enchantment of the innocent Christabel transforms the maiden from a state of innocence and purity to a state in which Christabel herself has taken on snake-like characteristics, hissing before her father and pleading for the rejection of Geraldine from the castle; Geraldine puts a curse or spell on Christabel which renders her powerless to reveal what has transpired in the bedchamber; and finally, through sexual enchantment of Sir Leoline, she leads him to reject his daughter. On the surface at least, we have a situation in which, as Edward Bostetter has pointed out,

> not only is the good invaded and violated without cause or warning, not only is it powerless to defend itself, but it is also involuntarily taking on in the second part of the poem the loathsome characteristics of the invader.[15]

But, on the other hand, it is difficult to see Geraldine as simply evil. In spite of such indications, complicating factors remain. For one thing, she does not appear to enjoy what she is doing and her malevolence, if this is the right word, is somewhat tempered by the pity she seems to feel for her victim. In the bedchamber she speaks to Christabel:

> All they who live in the upper sky,
> Do love you, holy Christabel!
> And you love them, and for their sake
> And for the good which me befel,
> Even I in my degree will try,
> Fair maiden, to requite you well.
> But now unrobe yourself; for I
> Must pray, ere yet in bed I lie. (I, 227-234)

These lines follow the terrible internal struggle between the enchantress and the invisible spirit of Christabel's mother, a struggle in which Geraldine emerges as the victor. Of course, the speech

---

[15] Edward E. Bostetter, *"Christabel:* The Vision of Fear", *PQ*, XXXVI (April, 1957), p. 183.

may be Geraldine's ironic commentary upon the situation. Having defeated the forces of good she can now comment sardonically upon the supposedly powerful forces which fail to protect the innocents who trust in them. And her promise to "requite" the maiden "well" may be a rather savage prediction of the actual evil she is about to perform. But it is really impossible to tell how ironically this speech is to be taken and the scene immediately following apparently suggests that the seduction is undertaken reluctantly. For here Geraldine struggles with herself and seems to steel herself to carry on with her appointed task.

> Ah what a stricken look was hers!
> Deep from within she seems half-way
> To lift some weight with sick assay,
> And eyes the maid and seeks delay; (I, 256-259)

Thus a kind of ambiguity exists in Coleridge's conception of the enchantress. The ambiguity is strengthened by Derwent Coleridge's observation, presumably based upon conversations with his father, that Geraldine is not a malignant being at all:

She is no witch or goblin or malignant being of any kind, but a spirit, executing her appointed task with the best of good will.

Somewhat aware of this duality in the character of Geraldine, Nethercott interprets the entire poem as "a romance of the preternatural". Geraldine is preternatural rather than supernatural: that is, a figure whose function is to produce ultimate good through the infliction of suffering. Coleridge's theory of the preternatural, upon which he bases the poem, Nethercott summarizes as follows:

There may be in the universe some kind of being, more divine than man, which is commissioned to care for the welfare of men and kingdoms. Pain may sometimes be necessary to dispel error but permanent good will comes from transitory evil.[16]

Furthermore, these beings are themselves probationers. They are on trial, working out a period of expiation for some past evil they have committed.

Geraldine, during the struggle with the mother's spirit, reminds

---

[16]   Arthur Nethercott, pp. 204-205.

her that she has been given power over the maiden for the term of her mission, suggesting certainly that more powerful forces in the universe than either Geraldine or the spirit of the mother are in some way responsible for what is about to occur. And the concept of expiation explains several details about Geraldine and her past. Whatever her crime had been, she is now paying for it and the symbol of her guilt is still in some way visible on her body. As Nethercott puts it, "her future depends on the successful accomplishment of her repugnant duty".[17]

Nethercott's interpretation, however, does not go quite far enough. The major difficulty with such an explanation is its close proximity to a rationalist explanation of evil. Coleridge would apparently be justifying the presence of human misery and unjustified suffering in terms of some mysterious cosmic plan, the ultimate consequences of which, man is unable to comprehend. The corruption and ultimate degradation of the innocent Christabel would be one link in some divine construct which will ultimately bring forth good. The burden of the argument in the poem would thus degenerate into an imaginative explanation of evil, a justification of God's ways to man.

But I wonder if the poem's meaning is so simple. If Geraldine functions in this poem as a sexual enchantress, if the forces she represents are in some way to be linked with the sexual and carnal, as I have suggested earlier, couldn't her ambiguous nature be explained as a reflection of Coleridge's ambivalent attitude toward these forces? As we saw in *Kubla Khan,* such forces are powerful, far too powerful to be constrained within the ordered, geometric pleasure dome of Xanadu. Furthermore, they are a threat to reason and order, particularly when confined. The eruption of the sacred river was not, I think, the result of apparently evil forces overcoming the forces of good, a catastrophe ultimately leading to the attainment of perfection through the agency of transitory evil. The dominant note throughout *Kubla Khan* is the note of inevitability. Given a particular act, in this case the construction of the pleasure dome circumscribing the sacred river, certain consequences fol-

---

[17]   Nethercott, p. 206.

low: i.e., the destruction of the pleasure dome. In a sense, this same pattern is evident in *Christabel*, and Geraldine's admission to the castle and seduction of the innocent has the same note of inevitability. Such inevitability may fill the conscious, masterful intellect with regret, and insofar as Coleridge's intellect, or in Potter's terms, "character", was in command during the composition of the poem, he perhaps laments the loss of innocence. But insofar as he recognizes the inevitability of such a loss, his attitude toward this demonic figure may be mixed.

That Christabel's loss of innocence is inevitable is suggested by the terms of her initial encounter with the enchantress. The opening lines of the poem, setting in precise detail the stage for the encounter, presents a conflict between the natural or the primitive, and the domestic, the tamed. The scene is within the castle, a castle we learn later, guarded by a massive, presumably indestructible gate: "The gate that was ironed within and without/ Where an army in battle array had marched out" (I, 127-128). The time is midnight, the witching hour, but emphasized in the first line is the man-made regular order of time by the clock. " 'Tis the middle of the night by castle clock." This brief reference to the regulated, logical order of time is picked up again in the second stanza where the "toothless mastiff bitch", domesticated, without teeth, and powerless, operates with a kind of mechanical, logical proficiency, echoing the chimes of the clock.

> She maketh answer to the clock,
> Four for the quarters and twelve for the hour;
> Ever and aye, by shine and shower,
> Sixteen short howls, not over loud. (I, 9-12)

This creature of the animal world, having lost all traces of her former primitive nature, functions as a kind of living clock. As we discover later, it is powerless to prevent Geraldine from entering the castle; in the role of guardian it is useless, unable to wake up, confining its dimly felt protest to an "angry moan".

This same mechanical quality of life in the castle is suggested again by the contrast in the first stanza between the two kinds of fowl, the owl and the cock: the wild and living owl in the forest, the tamed and domesticated cock in the castle. Momentarily the cock is awakened by the hooting of the owl; but just as the mastiff bitch subsides back into slumber when Geraldine passes, the cock's response to the wild owl is only momentary: "How drowsily it crew".

Furthermore, the master of the castle, Sir Leoline, the baron rich, is ill. As Christabel later informs Geraldine, "Sir Leoline is weak in health/ And may not well awakened be" (I, 118-120). The castle, then, at the time of the encounter, is a scene of perhaps once powerful forces now at rest, or in a state of decay. The "army in battle array had marched out"; what little life exists is in a dream-like state approaching death. The only sign of life is outside the castle.

The time of the year is April, however, and life is stirring:

> 'Tis a month before the month of May,
> And the Spring comes slowly up this way. (I, 21-22)

The encounter with Geraldine, then, co-incides with the coming of Spring, the universal symbol of life re-awakening, of rebirth and regeneration. And, of course, it is of the utmost significance that the encounter takes place outside the castle walls, in the natural world uncircumscribed by castle walls, or with "walls and towers . . . girdled round".

Christabel comes to the woods to pray for the health and safety of her lover; and as Basler has pointed out, she performs this act under the oak tree covered with mistletoe, the oak an obvious phallic symbol, the mistletoe a plant traditionally associated with fertility.[18] The poem suggests that such nocturnal excursions are not a part of Christabel's evening ritual:

> What makes her in the wood so late,
> A furlong from the castle gate? (I, 25-26)

She has been dreaming about her betrothed knight and has apparently felt compelled to offer up her prayers for his welfare somewhere other than within the presumably safe, enclosing walls of the castle. Thus it is in the world of nature, amid symbols of

---

[18]   Basler, p. 31.

fertility, in the month of April, while praying for her lover's safety, that Christabel first encounters the enchantress. In fact, Geraldine appears, it would seem, as a direct answer to the maiden's prayers.

> She kneels beneath the huge oak tree
> And in silence prayeth she
>
> The lady sprang up suddenly,
> The lovely lady, Christabel!
> It moaned as near, as near can be,
> But what it is she cannot tell. — (I, 35-42)

The results of this initial encounter turn out to be destructive – at least destructive of the castle life, including the death-like innocence of Christabel in the castle. We know that the lady in the woods will turn out to be the enchantress, the agent who will bring about the destruction of the civilized order. But none of this is suggested by the terms in which Geraldine is presented at this meeting in the woods.

Not, in fact, until the two have left the woods and approached the castle are any suspicions aroused that Geraldine is not the distressed maiden she claims to be. Only at the gates of the castle is Geraldine's supposedly evil nature first hinted at; she cannot enter the castle unassisted. According to popular legend, evil may not enter a home without the assistance of the inhabitants, and it is certainly clear that Coleridge wants us to think of this legend in relationship to the immediate scene. But why Christabel "carries" Geraldine over the threshold is not so clear. There are numerous ways in which Geraldine could have been invited to enter if Coleridge is only using the old legend in order to alert us to the evil nature of the lady from the forest.

But if at this time we interpret the significance of Geraldine not simply as an emissary of some evil force in the universe, but as a symbolic representation of erotic forces, other possibilities of interpretation are immediately opened up. Christabel's act of carrying the maiden over the threshold suggests a marriage scene; and considering what is about to transpire in her chamber, this is highly appropriate. Of course, in the seduction scene, Christabel is bride rather than bridegroom, and such a suggestion at this point

is not to be taken literally as an indication that Christabel is playing the role of bridegroom. It is merely that the idea of a marriage
is suggested or implied in this scene, preparing us for the ironic
"marriage" which is about to follow.

Geraldine, furthermore, is unable to pray to the Virgin, strongly
implying an inherently evil nature. But it is not the inability to
pray that is stressed here, although there is little doubt that such
an act would be out of keeping with an enchantress; the point
made is that she cannot pray to the Virgin and thus another
possibility of interpretation emerges. Quite obviously a Virgin
would be a poor object of devotion for a creature bent upon the
particular task that is hers: the deflowering of a Virgin.

And finally, capitalizing upon the old myth concerning the
ability of dogs and children to intuitively recognize evil, Coleridge
has the toothless guardian of the dying life in the castle, the mastiff
bitch, growl in her sleep as this intruder into the decaying scene
passes; and the fire which is almost dead, momentarily is rekindled
by her presence. However, it seems highly significant that each of
these clues to the evil nature of the enchantress can be symbolically interpreted as a clue to her sexual, perhaps life-giving nature as
well. Of course the mastiff bitch, whom we have previously seen
as a symbol of the dying life in the castle, will react to a threat
against what she symbolizes. And although the flames may
respond to the master of the flames, they are also means of
providing warmth and heat.

Geraldine is, I think, being presented here on two distinct
levels: on the one hand, she is the "evil" enchantress who, in a
world picture dominated by the forces within the castle, is bent
upon the destruction of innocence; on the other hand, she is the
personification of erotic, sexual forces entering the castle to perform their ministry through the seduction of Christabel. And our
attention is called to the fact that these two levels are distinct, not
necessarily one and the same, as perhaps a more traditional view
of such experience might suggest.

The duality in Geraldine's nature becomes even more clearly
apparent when she reaches the chamber. She sinks wearily to the
floor and Christabel, to revive her, offers a "cordial wine . . . of

virtuous powers" made by her mother "of wild flowers". At the mention of Christabel's mother, Geraldine asks if the mother will be likely to approve of Christabel's charitable action:

> And will your mother pity me,
> Who am a maiden most forlorn? (I, 194-195)

Christabel replies that her mother is dead and utters the seemingly irrelevant remark, in this context, that on her death-bed the mother had predicted,

> That she should hear the castle-bell
> Strike twelve upon my wedding-day. (I, 200-201)

Then, overcome with feeling, she utters the fervent plea, "Oh mother dear! that thou were here", and most strangely, "I would, said Geraldine, she were!" (I, 202-204).

There is something strange about this scene, preceding as it does the sudden appearance of the mother's spirit to offer ineffective battle to the enchantress. There seems to be no good reason for the mention of the mother's prophecy, unless it is meant to suggest, dramatically, some forthcoming action. And Geraldine's echo of Christabel's prayer seems totally out of place here, particularly if Geraldine is bent on some evil act.

I must admit that I do not completely understand this utterance of Geraldine's, but seen in the context of the entire scene, a tentative explanation can be offered. Symbolically, the seduction of Christabel is analogous to a wedding. The mother has predicted that she will *hear*, that is, be awakened, on Christabel's wedding day. In a sense, this is what happens. The mother's spirit is awakened by the clock striking twelve, and dismayed by the likelihood of an ironic fulfillment of her prediction, attempts to protect her daughter. Geraldine, knowing the power of a mother's prophecy, and also aware of the forthcoming seduction, wishes the mother to be there in order that the prophecy may indeed be fulfilled. As the events immediately following demonstrate, the mother's spirit is powerless to interfere and Geraldine, knowing this, welcomes the appearance of the ghost.

In this struggle with the mother's ghost, we see the inevitability of Christabel's loss of innocence. Nothing in the universe can save her. She has repeatedly offered up prayers: prayers for the safety of her lover, prayers to the Virgin, first for protection from the unknown before she meets Geraldine ("Mary, mother, save me now!"), second, prayers of thanksgiving for reaching the safety of the castle, prayers to the spirit of her mother. The narrator of the poem bursts into the action with an occasional plea for intervention: "Jesu, Maria, shield her well" (I, 54), "O shield her! shield sweet Christabel" (I, 254), and now, even the active intervention of her mother's spirit has no effect. The enchantress, borne along on the crest of some inevitable tide, tells the angry spirit:

> Off, wandering mother! Peak and pine!
> I have power to bid thee flee. (I, 205-206)
> . . .
> Off, woman, off! this hour is mine –
> Though thou her guardian spirit be,
> Off, woman, off! 'tis given to me. (I, 211-213)

Then she comforts the frightened Christabel who, witnessing the struggle with the invisible spirit, believes that the suffering of the mysterious lady has "wildered" her. Her words of comfort are, of course, the strange, half-threat, half-prophecy, that she is the emissary of those "who live in the upper sky" for whose sake she will attempt, even in her degree, to "requite" her well.

Again, if we can look at this scene and examine these words on a multidimensional level, in the context of the poem, not in the context of a particular value judgment about the subsequent action, there is really no reason to read Geraldine's lines as ironic. What follows may be a fall from innocence, but it is certainly not a fall lamented by the heavenly powers nor accompanied by dire predictions of total disaster. If traditional piety or obedience to a moral code ordained by God, or reliance upon a benevolent if strict deity, could save the maiden, then certainly everything possible has been done. But as this entire pre-seduction scene indicates, nothing can stop the enchantress from her work; and "they who live in the upper sky" must be seen as one of two things: either helpless against the forces represented by Geraldine, or acquiescing in the forthcoming events. What happens next may be terrible, but it is inevitable; we may be horrified, but our horror is futile. The innocent Christabel, like the impatient wedding guest, or the powerful Kubla, may represent a beautiful and ordered, a secure concept of human experience. But the wedding guest may not join the festivities until he has had his vision of horror; Kubla Khan cannot base his ordered universe on a dammed up sacred river; Christabel must face her Geraldine, alone in the chamber.

The disrobing scene following Geraldine's ambiguous prophecy, again moves in two contradictory directions. Christabel obeys the lady's command to disrobe:

> Her gentle limbs did she undress
> And lay down in her loveliness. (I, 237-238)

But her mind is too active to allow her immediate sleep; many thoughts, the exact nature of which is not defined, keep her from closing her eyes, and reclining upon her elbow, she watches the lady Geraldine undress.

The contortions of Geraldine as she disrobes are undoubtedly meant to suggest something sinister, brutal perhaps, and, above all, snake-like:

> Beneath the lamp the lady bowed,
> And slowly rolled her eyes around;
> Then drawing in her breath aloud,
> Like one that shuddered, she unbound
> The cincture from beneath her breast:
> Her silken robe, and inner vest,
> Dropt to her feet, and full in view,
> Behold! her bosom and half her side –
> A sight to dream of, not to tell!
> O shield her! shield sweet Christabel! (I, 245-254)

And certainly Coleridge meant to suggest that the sight of Geraldine's "bosom and half her side" was terrifying, particularly to the innocent Christabel, who is intently watching the scene from her bed like a waiting bride. Coleridge's first version of the poem defined with more precision the physical details of Geraldine's revelation:

> Behold her bosom and half her side
> All lean and old and foul of hue . . .

In this original draft his conception focused primarily on the horror. But the first version of any poem may contain lines, details, concrete and specific images, which when seen in the context of the finished poem must be scrapped. The interesting question here is why Coleridge changed the much more concrete image of the enchantress's bosom, which leaves no room for ambiguous interpretation, to the far more abstract and less poetic line, "a sight to dream of, not to tell".

The fact is, if we bear in mind the ambiguity in the presentation of Geraldine so far, wouldn't the specific image of physical horror tend to destroy this ambiguity? Perhaps the poet realizes that to define too closely, to establish Geraldine as a traditional foul and witch-like hag, would do violence to the counter-flow of responses he has created around the figure so far.

Thus perhaps the image is deliberately blurred as the poem undergoes revision. The horror of the scene is suggested in the sinister movements of Geraldine as she disrobes, and the following lines emphasize it even more. Geraldine refers to her naked bosom, the "sight to dream of, not to tell" as the source of her power:

> In the touch of this bosom there worketh a spell,
> Which is lord of thy utterance, Christabel!
> Thou knowest tonight and will know to-morrow,
> This mark of my shame, this seal of my sorrow.
> (I, 267-270)

In the process of casting the spell which will make Christabel unable to tell what happens in the chamber, the lady's ambiguous nature is again emphasized. Her powers, as sinister as they may be, rest in this enigmatic and vague sight which must remain a secret. The lady herself takes no great delight in being possessed of such powers – they are the mark and seal of her *shame* and *sorrow,* and she recognizes it.

In the conclusion of Part I, all the events of the night come to a climax. By specific suggestion and detail, Coleridge makes it unambiguously clear, I think, that the enchantment of Christabel is sexual. The mission of Geraldine is a mission of sexual seduction.

The conclusion begins with the picture of perfect innocence – the Christabel who prayed at the old oak tree:

> Her slender palms together prest,
> Heaving sometimes on her breast;
> Her face resigned to bliss or bale –
> Her face, oh call it fair not pale,
> And both blue eyes more bright than clear,
> Each about to have a tear. (I, 286-291)

Undoubtedly, this had been, in the poet's words, "a lovely sight to see", as the pleasure dome "was a miracle of rare device". Here is the image of perfect trust, perfect faith, perfect innocence, if not perfect vision – "eyes more bright than clear".

But the next stanza presents a new image of Christabel:

> With open eyes (ah woe is me!)
> Asleep, and dreaming fearfully,
> Fearfully dreaming, yet I wis,
> Dreaming that alone, which is –
> O sorrow and shame! Can this be she,
> The lady, who knelt at the old oak tree?
>   (I, 292-297)

Her eyes are open now, even though she is apparently asleep and dreaming. But the dream is not a dream; what she thinks has been a dream, a fearful dream, is real. What she sees is reality; her eyes may perhaps now be described as more "clear" than bright. And the poet, the narrator, is aghast. Without the actual details of seduction being presented, we realize that a transformation has come over Christabel. The image of innocence, "the lady, who knelt at the old oak tree", as she now is, awake and aware, evokes the cry "O sorrow and shame": the verbal symbols of Geraldine's power. The "sorrow and shame" of Geraldine has now been transferred to Christabel; and the enchantress, "the worker of these harms", having performed her task, slumbers peacefully "still and mild", her arm around the maiden, who is presumably wide awake now, but in this dream-like state of perceptiveness.

Something has occurred to produce this state, something perhaps as unmentionable as the "sight to dream of, not to tell". The following stanza with its image of the setting and rising stars, tells us that Geraldine, whose arms "have been the lovely lady's prison", has had her will: one hour was hers, and now it is past.

But the hour has been a successful one, and the night-birds in the forest, who had remained silent during the fateful hour, now burst into a jubilant rejoicing:

> From clif and tower, tu-whoo! tu-whoo!
> Tu-whoo! tu-whoo! from wood and fell!

Geraldine, the mistress of the night and the forces of nature, has succeeded in her mission, and the world outside bursts into tumultuous celebration.

The scene shifts back to Christabel's bed:

> And see! the lady Christabel
> Gathers herself from out her trance;
> Her limbs relax, her countenance
> Grows sad and soft; the smooth thin lids
> Close o'er her eyes; and tears she sheds —
> Large tears that leave the lashes bright!
> And oft the while she seems to smile
> As infants at a sudden light! (I, 311-318)

Basler finds that these lines describe a sexual "after-rest" emphasizing the obvious sexual nature of Christabel's experience with Geraldine.[19] Surely this is not too strong. I think Coleridge could have gone no further in pointing out the sexual nature of this scene without having his poem banned in 19th century England. Christabel, through her encounter with the mysterious lady, has been deflowered; this is the climax toward which everything in the poem so far has been leading.

As Christabel falls asleep she smiles and weeps,

> ... like a youthfull hermitess
> Beauteous in a wilderness
> Who, praying always, prays in sleep. (I, 320-322)

She is no longer the innocent, the protected virgin; she may be alone in a wilderness, but she is alive. The "blood so free/ Comes back and tingles in her feet." In sleep, at least, she momentarily may feel secure, and the poem puts this sense of security in the form of a question:

19   Basler, pp. 38-39.

> What if her guardian spirit 'twere,
> What if she knew her mother near? (I, 327-328)

But this is only a possibility, somewhat remote, for the mother's spirit has already been routed in the battle with Geraldine. The first part of the poem ends with the hollow, perhaps ironic, assurance that:

> . . . saints will aid if men will call;
> For the blue sky bends over all! (I, 330-331)

Had the poem ended at this point, there would be little difficulty in recognizing the ambiguity of feeling which Coleridge displays toward this demonic force moving with inevitable power toward the destruction of the ordered universe man tries to construct upon innocence. However, there is no doubt that the events of Part II seem to cast some doubt upon Geraldine's apparent ambiguous nature. For if the seduction of Christabel is to be interpreted as a release from innocence, and the influence of Geraldine upon the maiden is not malign, how do we account for the strange transformation of Christabel in Part II? For in this section of the poem, Christabel begins to take on snake-like characteristics, pleading hysterically for the expulsion of Geraldine from the castle.

When she awakes in the morning, Christabel has no immediate feelings of repulsion for her seducer. She suffers only from a vague feeling of guilt:

> "Sure I have sinned!" said Christabel,
> "Now heaven be praised if all be well!" (II, 381-382)

For Geraldine, apparently refreshed after her night's rest, seems once more to be only the beautiful lady Christabel had rescued from the forest. In perfect trust, apparently, Christabel leads the enchantress to Sir Leoline, who greets her warmly. Learning that she is the daughter of an old friend, he vows revenge upon those who had abducted the fair lady. At the thought of the injury to the honor of Geraldine, he wishes to meet these "recreant traitors" in his tourney court,

> ". . . that there and then
> I may dislodge their reptile souls

From the bodies and forms of men!"
He spake: his eye in lightning rolls. (II, 441-444)

This is the first sign of any life in the Baron; Geraldine's effect is
to rouse him from his illness and apathy: "O then the Baron forgot
his age/ His noble heart swelled high with rage." (II, 431-432)

The opening of Part II has emphasized once more the death-
like state of the castle. The morning, as described outside the
chamber in which Geraldine and Christabel lie, is not a time of
reawakening. No birds are singing, no cocks are crowing; life, such
as it is, in the castle begins with the slow, funereal tolling of the
"matin bell" knelling "us back to a world of death". The bells
peal slowly and mournfully;

                    ... the sacristan,
        Who duly pulls the heavy bell,
        Five and forty beads must tell
        Between each stroke – a warning knell. (II, 339-342)

This has been the custom and the law since the Baron's wife had
died. The gloom and death-like atmosphere of the castle at night
are apparently continued during the day. The castle awakens from
a death-like night to a death-like day. In fact, the only break in
this scene of unmitigated gloom is the echo of the bells which fills
up the long, mournful spaces in between the strokes:

        In Langdale Pike and Witch's Lair,
        And Dungeon-ghyll so foully rent,
        With ropes of rock and bells of air
        Three sinful sextons' ghosts are pent,
        Who all give back, one after t'other,
        The death-note to their living brother;
        And oft too, by the knell offended,
        Just as their one! two! three! is ended,
        The devil mocks the doleful tale
        With a merry peal from Borodale. (II, 350-359)

This elaborate conceit is far more than a decorative embellishment;
for the same ambiguous attitude toward the life-in-death that
prevails in the castle is indicated again. The only sign of life is the
mocking echo from outside the castle, the "three sinful sextons"
filling in the spaces with their "ropes of rock and bells of air". And

the devil himself joins in the tumult from outside, mocking the doleful tale of the bells with "merry peals".

It is the "merry peals" from the devil that awaken Geraldine, appropriately enough; but, more to the point, it is Geraldine's influence upon the Baron that causes him to step out of his melancholy pursuit of death. The demonic forces become identified with the only signs of life in the castle, just as Geraldine is in opposition to the trustful innocence of Christabel.

But, as we observe the result of the loss of innocence, there seems to be little doubt that in its immediate effect upon Christabel, it is a change for the worse. For when the Baron embraces Geraldine, after assuring her that he will avenge her abduction, Christabel remembers something of the night before:

> The vision of fear, the touch and pain!
> She shrunk and shuddered, and saw again –
>
> (II, 453-454)

> Again she saw that bosom old,
> Again she felt that bosom cold,
> And drew in her breath with a hissing sound.
>
> (II, 457-459)

The snake-like hissing sound from the lips of Christabel is shocking and totally unexpected. That she should recall the details of her night with Geraldine, even recall them now with loathing and repulsion, recalling only the horror of Geraldine's mark of sorrow and shame is accountable enough; but that the recollection should produce this uncharacteristic hissing from the lips of the "gentle maid", suggests certainly the beginnings of some transformation in Christabel.

Although the hissing is audible, for the Baron turns "wildly around" at the sound, there is no indication that any visible change in Christabel's appearance has taken place. The knight sees nothing

> ... but his own sweet maid
> With eyes upraised, as one that prayed.
> The touch, the sight, had passed away
> And in its stead that vision blest,

Which comforted her after-rest
While in the lady's arms she lay,
Had put a rapture in her breast,
And on her lips and o'er her eyes
Spread smiles like light! (II, 461-471)

Something really diabolical underlies this quick juxtaposition of images: Christabel, recalling the horror of the night, hisses like a snake; but following so quickly upon the image of the snake, so quickly as to be almost a simultaneous response, is the image of angelic innocence. This is not to say that Christabel deliberately covers up her guilt; both the look of innocence and the hissing sound come through no act of volition. But the effect of the images produces a moment of suspicion, an indication that all is not as it seems. For the fact is that the hissing has emerged from lips of the Baron's "own sweet maid/ With eyes upraised, as one that prayed".

And as we read further, we discover that the look of innocence springs from the same source as the sound of evil, the recollection of the previous night. The "vision of fear" which springs from the recollection of the horror is supplanted by the "vision blest,/ Which comforted her after-rest/ While in the lady's arms she lay." Geraldine is responsible then for both visions, underscoring again the mixture of good and evil which she represents.

This same pattern is struck again after Bard Bracy's account of his strange prophetic dream. This dream of a dove, obviously meant to symbolize Christabel, attacked by a small, almost invisible snake, is noteworthy in several respects; the details describing the attack suggest, not so much a snake attempting to strangle a dove, as two lovers embraced in the sex act:

... I saw a bright green snake
Coiled around its wings and neck.
Green as the herbs on which it couched,
Close by the dove's its head it crouched;
And with the dove it heaves and stirs,
Swelling its neck as she swelled hers! (II, 549-554)

The dream occurs at midnight, the time of the meeting of the woods, for "the clock was echoing in the tower". And, of course, the emphasis upon the snake's color, its greenness matching the green herbs, suggests again the natural world of the forest which, as we have seen, is the world Geraldine appears from.

Bard Bracy, the poet-priest concerned with the spiritual welfare of the castle's inhabitants, sees the dream only as an indication of something unholy in the woods, threatening Christabel. But Sir Leoline interprets the dream as a threat to Geraldine, which in an ironic sense it is. (The Bard will be trying, ineffectively we assume, to chase the evil spirits away with "music strong and saintly song".) Sir Leoline refers to the enchantress as "Lord Roland's beauteous dove" and vows, as he has vowed before, to protect her from harm:

> "With arms more strong than harp or song
> Thy sire and I will crush the snake!"
> He kissed her forehead as he spake. (II, 570-572)

And again, at the knight's embrace, we have the snake motif struck, this time in the actions of both Geraldine and Christabel. Geraldine, after the embrace, looks "askance" at Christabel, and the maiden sees the "vision of fear" again.

> A snake's small eye blinks dull and shy;
> And the lady's eyes they shrunk in her head,
> Each shrunk up to a serpent's eye,
> And with somewhat of malice, and more of dread,
> At Christabel she looked askance! –
> One moment – and the sight was fled! (II, 583-589)

The effect of this look upon Christabel is hypnotic; again she is transformed:

> But Christabel in a dizzy trance
> Stumbling on the unsteady ground
> Shuddered aloud, with a hissing sound. (II, 590-592)

While Geraldine, assured that her power over the maiden is secure, returns her attention to the knight.

> Full of wonder and full of grief,
> She rolled her large, bright eyes divine
> Wildly on Sir Leoline. (II, 594-596)

Christabel, in the dizzy trance, full of the vision of serpent eyes, slowly takes on more of the serpent characteristics.

> The maid, devoid of guile and sin,
> I know not how, in fearful wise,
> So deeply had she drunken in
> That look, those shrunken serpent eyes,
> That all her features were resigned
> To this sole image in her mind:
> And passively did imitate
> That look of dull and treacherous hate! (II, 599-606)

As in the first such description of Christabel's transformation, a contrast is drawn between this "look of dull and treacherous hate", which Christabel "imitates" or "pictures" with "forced unconscious sympathy", and the innocent eyes that contain no hint of this look:

> And thus she stood, in dizzy trance,
> Still picturing that look askance
> With forced unconscious sympathy
> Full before her father's view —
> As far as such a look could be
> In eyes so innocent and blue. (II, 607-612)

The scene ends with Christabel throwing herself at the Baron's feet and imploring him in the name of her mother's soul to send Geraldine away. The Baron, enraged at his daughter's inhospitable action, turns away from "his own sweet maid" and leads forth "the lady Geraldine". The enchantress has, in fact, taken over the castle; she has, in the context of the poem as we now have it, extended her influence over the Baron as well as the innocent girl. But the reader is left in a quandary about how he is to respond to this final triumph.

For Geraldine's seduction of Christabel is the symbolic image of innocence destroyed; and the destruction of innocence has brought with it the transformation of Christabel, against her will, to a state similar to the demonic. But the moral implications here are confused and ambiguous — the demonic images are constantly superimposed upon the images of innocence; the corruption of Christabel has accompanied the revival of life in the castle; the civilized, organized and domestic world has been subverted, but the natural, primitive world, the source of life, has been revived. Geraldine, like the Ancient Mariner, may be a figure to evoke fear, loathing, even horror, to the eyes of the quiet world. She may indeed be identified with the devil. But, perhaps, and of this I am not completely certain, the change she produces in Christabel is in some way equivalent to the change in the Wedding Guest. Perhaps the loss of innocence is equivalent to the gaining of vision. Christabel's eyes are clearer now; and perhaps corruption is necessary in this world in order to live, and in order to *see*.

The conclusion to Part II is, I think, confusing in more ways than in syntax. So far as I can see, the conclusion has nothing to do with the dramatic movement of the poem. I fail to see how the words in any way relate to the action of any of the characters. But the argument of these perplexing lines has a great deal to do with the argument of the poem as I have interpreted it. They express a realization, perhaps a revelation, of the narrator which is almost too horrible to be accepted, but which nonetheless seems to be true. And this revelation is closely connected to the revelation which the dramatic action of the poem has led us to see.

The conclusion begins by presenting the image of innocence, the little dancing child with "red, round cheeks", the sight of which "fills the father's eyes with light". But the father, who no longer lives in this innocent world, in order to express his love for the child, must do it with "words of unmeant bitterness". The child's world must be broken in upon; love must express itself in words which seem the opposite of love:

> Perhaps 'tis tender too and pretty
> At each wild word to feel within
> A sweet recoil of love and pity. (II, 670-672)

There seems the possibility that love can only be expressed through these "wild words" of "unmeant bitterness"; and, even worse, perhaps even the emotion itself springs from such an inappropriate source:

> And what, if in a world of sin
> (O sorrow and shame should this be true!)
> Such giddiness of heart and brain
> Comes seldom save from rage and pain. (II, 673-676)

The father, "in a world of sin", is thus the destroyer of the child's world; in order to save the child he must destroy its innocence.

And, by implication, the child must become aware of this world where love does not exist except in the company of rage, pain, and bitterness. The child, when it is mature, will share this corrupt, but real, knowledge.

This, it seems to me, is the argument of the poem, up to this point. Christabel's pious innocence is not enough; she must be corrupted in order to exist in the corrupt world. And all defenses erected to protect her from corruption serve only to deny life itself. The change of Christabel is the sign of her awakening: an awakening to life and to reality. The poet may well lament, "O sorrow and shame should this be true"; but in the context of the poem, it seems to be true enough.

I do not mean to argue that Coleridge himself is consciously and deliberately trying to suggest in logical terms that what has happened to Christabel is good. In fact, it is quite unambiguously clear that the image we have of Christabel at the end of Part II is a horrible one. She may be awake; but like the ancient mariner, she has paid a high price for such an awakening. And although the loss of innocence may be an inevitable consequence of being alive, it is perhaps too much for the conscious, public character of the poet to accept.

I think this may have a great deal to do with Coleridge's failure to finish the poem. Granted that all such speculations must be extremely tentative, it nonetheless makes a kind of sense to recognize that any conscious awareness of the symbolic possibilities of the poem could have put Coleridge into a state of poetic paralysis. On the one hand he had created an image of life restored through the influence of the erotic; on the other hand he had shown the ultimate effects of this lifegiving force to be horrifying. He is caught between his own ambivalent feelings toward the erotic and is unable to resolve the ambivalence in a work of art, as he did in *Kubla Khan.*

As a result, *Christabel* fails as a coherent work of art, as *Kubla Khan* does not. The moral center, the base from which the contradictory and ambivalent feelings can operate and which ultimately can resolve them, is missing. The attitudes of the poem toward the erotic remain not merely ambivalent, but confused. And since

Coleridge apparently could hit upon no appropriate method of resolving the confusion without destroying the ambivalence, the poem remained unfinished.

The projected ending which would have had Christabel's lover returning from the wars to chase Geraldine from the castle and rescue his beloved would completely destroy the tone of the first part of the poem. For Christabel has already been rescued, in symbolic terms, by Geraldine. The defeat of the forces of Eros by another representative of the same force would not make much sense, even symbolically. But a total victory for Geraldine would involve far more Freudian awareness, I suspect, than even Coleridge possessed, since in traditional terms a witch is still a witch and associated with evil.

We see, then, in Coleridge an attitude toward the erotic which is mixed and ambivalent, one that is sharply in contrast with the traditional. Not that poets before him had never shown ambiguous feelings toward the erotic, nor that traditional Christian poets had never shown the same kind of compulsions. But Coleridge lacks the conviction that the erotic and the irrational are in any way necessarily opposed to the good, with their roots in a Satanic plot to destroy man. He may have the desire to believe in an ordered and rational universe, but he does not operate from a firm assumption that such a universe exists or can exist contrary to the nature of man.

In fact, for Coleridge the values of a God-centered universe seem inappropriate for man's world; the direct result is the ambivalence displayed in these poems, an ambivalence toward the forces of reason and the forces of passion as they affect man's life in the world.

III

THE PHYSICAL BASIS OF LOVE IN SHELLEY'S
ALASTOR AND *EPIPSYCHIDION*

One problem in the way of a modern reader's acceptance of
Shelley's poetry is the poet's apparent rejection of the physical basis
of love. To many readers, the comments of Newman I. White sum
up Shelley's habit of ignoring the forms of physical love and
concentrating upon a Platonic ideal:

Shelleyan love is simply an intense longing for complete sympathy.
The highest love between two human beings was their common perception, in each other, of the shadow of intellectual beauty and their
common aspiration toward a more complete unity with intellectual
Beauty.[1]

Essentially the same notion is expressed by Floyd Stovall when he
argues that Shelley

accepted the doctrine that the love of the ideally beautiful conducts
to virtue, wisdom and happiness, and endeavored at all times to subject himself to its dominion.[2]

One is led to believe, if we accept such views of Shelley, that none
of his love poetry is directly concerned with sex and that whenever
he treats the subject of love between man and woman, he does not
include within his vision actual physical union. Shelleyan love
apparently tries to transcend the sex act; his ideal of perfection
appears to be a universe in which a union of lovers would be only
a spiritual mixing of souls and essences, with little or no touching
of bodies.

[1] Newman I. White, *Shelley*, II (New York, A. A. Knopf, 1940), pp. 443-
444.
[2] Floyd Stoval, *Desire and Restraint in Shelley* (Durham, N.C., Duke
University Press, 1931), p. 144.

Now there is much in Shelley's poetry to support such a view. The first encounter of the lovers in *Epipsychidion* is a meeting of spirits:

> There was a Being whom my spirit oft
> Met on its visioned wanderings, far aloft,
> In the clear golden prime of my youth's dawn,
> Upon the fairy isles of sunny lawn . . .
>   .   .   .
> She met me, robed in such exceeding glory,
> That I beheld her not. (190-200)[3]

The spirit of the poet-narrator falls in love with the mere apprehension of beauty, the pure spirit of the lady. The same elements of the non-physical are present to an even greater extent in *Alastor*, where the poet-protagonist ignores all earthly incarnations of female beauty and can love only a dream-maiden, one who appears to him in a vision.

Such an idealization of love is found in some of his prose pieces as well. The prose fragment *On Love*, defines the emotion of love as follows:

It is that powerful attraction toward all that we conceive or fear, or hope beyond ourselves . . . the bond and sanction which connects not only man with man, but with everything that exists.[4] (p. 170)

In the *Defense of Poetry*, he defines it once more:

The great secret of morals is love – a going out of our own nature, and an identification of ourselves with the beautiful which exists in thought, action, or person not our own. (pp. 282-283)

And finally in his *Discourse on the Manners of the Ancient Greeks Relative to the Subject of Love*, it is called "a universal thirst for communion, not only of the senses, but of our whole nature, intellectual, imaginative, and sensitive". (p. 220).

Taking these various definitions out of context one can easily

---

[3]   All citations to Shelley's poetry are to *The Poems of Shelley* (London, Oxford University Press, 1960).
[4]   All citations to Shelley's prose are to *Shelley's Prose: The Trumpet of a Prophecy*, ed. David L. Clark (Albuquerque, University of New Mexico Press, 1954).

form the notion that Shelley rejected the whole idea of any biological basis of love. White, in fact, sees Shelley as holding in utter contempt that kind of love referred to in the lyric addressed to either Emilia Viviani or Jane Williams.

> One word is too often profaned
> For me to profane it,
> One feeling too often disdained
> For thee to disdain it.
>
> I can give not what men call love,
> But wilt thou accept not
> The worship the heart lifts above
> And the Heavens reject not.

Erotic love, according to White, is "what men call love". It is "the biological and sensational function of love ... a different thing from spiritual love, on a far different, and inferior plane of living".[5]

However, as Edward E. Bostetter has pointed out, there is no real evidence to support the notion that Shelley drew any distinction in kind between erotic or sensual love and spiritual love.[6] What White and others seem to miss is that Shelleyan love always begins with the physical, and is in fact rooted in the physical world. Shelley recognized that the exalted, transcendent, ethereal love which may indeed be the center of all moral conduct, starts in a contemplation of earthly beauty. The distinction, if indeed it is a distinction at all, is a distinction in quality, not in kind. Reading further in *On Love*, we find that Shelley ties his spirituality to a definite, earthly manifestation of beauty:

If we reason, we would be understood; if we imagine, we would the airy children of our brain were born anew within anothers; if we feel, we would that another's nerves should vibrate to our own, that the beams of their eyes should kindle at once and mix and melt into our own, that lips of motionless ice should not reply to lips quivering and burning with the heart's best blood. This is Love. (p. 170)

[5]   Newman I. White, p. 443.
[6]   Edward E. Bostetter, "Shelley and the Mutinous Flesh", *Texas Studies in Language and Literature*, I (1959), pp. 203-213.

Love then is not centered around adoration of something abstract. It is intimately grounded in an earthly representation of the ideal. We need other people, other human beings with nerves and eyes and lips. The appeal here is for human sympathy, not divine illumination.

The essay goes on to argue that when we are unable to find this sympathy and understanding in a human being, we look for it in the non-human objects of the natural world:

Hence in solitude, or in that deserted state when we are surrounded by human beings, and yet they sympathize not with us, we love the flowers, the grass, the waters, and the sky. (p. 170)

The central idea of the essay seems to be simply this: man needs human sympathy, a sense of being understood and loved by another human being. When he receives it, he feels an overpowering, almost transcendent emotion inspired by this sensual apprehension of earthly beings and/or objects. It need not, and perhaps cannot, take place in an abstract vacuum inhabited by purely imaginative phantoms. Love may lead to a sense of liberation from the actual world, but it begins with the physical.

The *Discourse on . . . the Ancient Greeks . . .*, when examined closely, shows the same attitude. It is an attempt to justify, perhaps even condone, the homosexual activities of the ancient Greeks. The reason for this homosexuality is to be found, Shelley thinks, in the degraded position of women in Greek society. Consistent with his point in the essay *On Love*, that love is more than simple corporeal union, he argues that the Greek woman because of her low status, education and sensibility, was fit only for cohabitation to preserve the race:

They possessed, except with extraordinary exceptions, the habits and qualities of slaves. They were probably not extremely beautiful; at least there was no such disproportion in the attractions of the external form between the female and the male sex among the Greeks as exists among the modern Europeans. They were certainly devoid of that moral and intellectual loveliness with which the acquisition of knowledge and the cultivation of sentiment animates as with another life of overpowering grace the lineaments and the gestures of every form which it inhabits. Their eyes could not have been deep and intricate from the workings of the mind and could have entangled no heart in soul-enwoven labyrinths. (p. 220)

We must realize, he goes on, that the Greeks, at least the males, were civilized, and as civilization develops

the gratification of the senses is no longer all that is sought in sexual connexion. It soon becomes a very small part of that profound and complicated sentiment, which we call love, which is rather the universal thirst for a communion not merely of the senses, but of our whole nature, intellectual, imaginative and sensitive. The sexual impulse, which is only one, and often a small part of these claims, serves, from its obvious and external nature, as a kind of type or expression of the rest, a common basis, an acknowledged and visible link. (pp. 203-204)

Thus the Greek male seeking some human object who could comprehend and understand the "intellectual" as well as the sexual claims of love but "deprived of their natural object", tried to find a "compensation and a substitute", the direct result of which was that "beautiful persons of the male sex became the object of that sort of feelings, which are only cultivated at the present as towards females" (p. 221).

Throughout the *Discourse*, then, runs the theme of the inevitability of sexual passion and the necessity of finding in earthly form some other being who can realize the complexity of the sexual act.

"The act itself is nothing", he exclaims; but in the process of pronouncing the nothingness of it, he recognizes not only its existence but also its importance in the complex emotions of love. A Shelley such as some interpreters have discovered, separating the biology of love from its spirituality, would have no need to make such a detailed defense. But aware of the dependence of ideal love upon sexual feelings, he uses the practices of the Greeks to define and further clarify his own attitudes and belief that ideal love is indivisible from corporeal love; although the ideal involves a constant searching for some sexual partner who can involve our whole nature rather than simply the corporeal part of it, the sex act is an act by which a qualitatively higher experience is reached. In itself it is nothing, but without it there is nothing. It is a "kind of type or expression of the rest, a common basis, an acknowledged and visible link. Still it is a claim which even derives a strength not its own from the accessory circumstances which surround it and one which our nature thirsts to satisfy" (p. 220).

This awareness of and dependence upon the sensual basis of love becomes one of the important elements in Shelley's love poetry, an element that seems to me to have been pretty much disregarded by many critics. Although it is perfectly obvious that such a poem as *Alastor* deals with the subject of love, widespread disagreement exists as to whether or not the love by which the young poet-protagonist in the poem is possessed is an ideal, abstract love, dissociated from the senses, or, as the poem itself states, "the spirit of sweet *human* [my italics] love", a sensual, sexually based love. In other words, did Shelley intend the poem to depict the story of an ideal youth whose quest for an ideal maiden resulted in his tragic but somehow glorious destruction, or did he mean that the protagonist is being punished for some fatal flaw in his otherwise peerless character? Carlos Baker is convinced that the poem is

the story of a youth who took natural philosophy as his province, and was happy enough until he suddenly awoke to the thought that he needed sympathetic association with an ideal. Having united into a single idealized but pleasantly voluptuous image all of the wonderful, wise, and beautiful ideas known to him, he became passionately attached to his creation.[7]

The poem is simply a quest-poem; there is no avenging spirit of any kind in the poem itself, according to Baker, and there is therefore no necessity for us to look for, or be aware of any sensual basis for the poet's dream maiden – she is pure spirit, pure ideal, pure vision.

O. W. Campbell also denies that any thought of human, earthly love informs the poem; the poet-protagonist, like Shelley himself, was totally divorced from the mundane conditions of earthly life, and this is his glory. His untimely death is not a punishment for

[7] Carlos Baker, *Shelley's Major Poetry: The Fabric of a Vision* (Princeton, Princeton University Press, 1948), p. 43.

his neglect; it is like Galahad's quest for the Holy Grail, ending as it must in an early death.[8]

These attempts to idealize the love theme of the poem certainly do not represent the prevailing view of the poem. Most readers recognize that in some way the youth is culpable, that the title of the poem, *Alastor* – the name of a Greek avenging spirit – as well as the Preface, in which Shelley is fairly specific in outlining the theme, lead us to see the youth as having committed some grievous sin against human nature. For according to the Preface, the theme of *Alastor* is that a complete concentration upon high and lofty ideals brings with it an inevitable avenging fury which ultimately makes such idealistic quests meaningless. The Preface states of the poet that

so long as it is possible for his desires to point toward objects . . . infinite and unmeasured, he is joyous, and tranquil, and self-possessed. But the period arrives when these objects cease to suffice. His mind is at length suddenly awakened and thirsts for intercourse with an intelligence similar to itself. . . . The Poet's self-centered seclusion was avenged by the furies of an irresistible passion pursuing him to speedy ruin.

However, the Preface continues, those who are never inspired to search beyond the finite and the earthly are doomed to a fate worse than the Poet's. Although the Poet's habit of avoiding the world of humanity was reprehensible,even more reprehensible are those who never make the attempt to move beyond the physical:

Among those who attempt to exist without human sympathy, the pure and tender-hearted perish through the intensity and passion of their search after its communities, when the vacancy of their spirit suddenly makes itself felt. All else, selfish, blind, and torpid, are those unforeseeing multitudes who constitute, together with their own, the lasting misery and loneliness of the world. Those who love not their fellow-beings live unfruitful lives, and prepare for their old age a miserable grave.

Thus the theme of the poem is as follows: The "selfish, blind and torpid" are those without ideals, those like the Greek females men-

8   O. W. Campbell, *Shelley and the Unromantics* (London, Methuen and Co., Ltd., 1924), pp. 189-191.

tioned in the *Discourse* who through lack of education, lack of refinement, admit the existence of nothing more than the actualities of the real world. Those others, aware of the possibilities beyond the purely biological and physical, may try to live unattached to the real world because nothing in this world of the actual satisfies them. As Carl Grabo states it, perhaps the Shelleyean ideal, the golden mean

is to be found . . . in those who, aware of otherworldly ideals, find in them inspiration to human love and sympathy in this mortal life. Both to misanthrope and idealist there is a form of selfishness which begets unhappiness and death.[9]

It is unnecessary to trace the critical battle over whether or not the poem actually sticks to the theme presented in the preface. I think my analysis of certain sections of the poem will show that it is largely consistent with this theme; and for much of what follows I am largely dependent upon such critics as Harold L. Hoffman,[10] Carl Grabo, and Evan K. Gibson,[11] whose analyses of the poem seem to be headed in the right direction.

Just as Shelley's prose indicated that to him all love, even the most idealized forms of it, is firmly rooted in the senses, we find that the values celebrated in *Alastor* are the values of a necessary commitment to the things of earth. The invocation makes this commitment to the earth perfectly clear:

> Earth, ocean, air, beloved brotherhood!
> If our great Mother has imbued my soul
> With aught of natural piety to feel
> Your love, and recompense the boon with mine;
> If dewy morn, and odorous noon, and even,
> With sunset and its gorgeous ministers,
> And solemn midnight's tingling silentness;
> If autumn's hollow sighs in the sere wood,
> And winter robing with pure snow and crowns

[9]   Carl Grabo, *The Magic Plant: The Growth of Shelley's Thought* (Chapel Hill, University of North Carolina Press, 1936), p. 174.
[10]   Harold L. Hoffman, *An Odyssey of the Soul: Shelley's "Alastor"* (New York, Columbia University Press, 1933).
[11]   Evan K. Gibson, "Alastor: A Reinterpretation", *PMLA*, LXII (1947), pp. 1022-1045.

Of starry ice the grey grass and bare boughs;
If spring's voluptuous pantings when she breathes
Her first sweet kisses, have been dear to me;
If no bright bird, insect, or gentle beast
I consciously have injured, but still loved
And cherished these my kindred; then forgive
This boast, beloved brethren, and withdraw
No portion of your wonted favour now! (1-17)

This is no invocation to any abstract deity, but a prayer to the *things* of earth to inspire him. The poet is attached to them: he feels a love for them, and they return this love. This invocation is a catalogue of natural, earth-oriented things to which our senses can respond. The "dewey morn", the "odorous noon", the "solemn midnight's tingling silentness", the "hollow sighs" of autumn, and winter with its snow and ice robing the "grey grass and bare boughs". Spring with its "voluptuous paintings" and kisses, is described as a lover might describe a mistress.

The invocation continues, addressing now the "Mother of this unfathomable world!" presumably the "great Mother" of the second line, the metaphorical mother of the poet as well as all other natural phenomena, the earth, the ocean, the air, the "beloved brotherhood", of which the poet is one. The poet states his qualifications as narrator: he, like the poet in the poem, has tried to wrest the secrets of nature from this "mother", "hoping to still these obstinate questionings/ Of thee and thine, by forcing some lone ghost/ Thy messenger, to render up the tale/ Of what we are" (26-29). His attempt, unlike that of the protagonist of the poem, has been unsuccessful, however: "ne'er yet/ Thou has unveiled thy inmost sanctuary" (37-38). Still he has learned enough to love and in some small measure, to appreciate the mystery of the "Great Parent". He has searched, but has given up the search for an absolute knowledge, and

                     ... serenely now
        And moveless, as a long-forgotten lyre
        Suspended in the solitary dome
        Of some mysterious and deserted fane,
        I wait thy breath ... (41-45)

He is content, now, to play the role of a passive instrument, allow-

ing the breath of the "Great Parent" to create the song he is about
to produce – a song that will

> ... modulate with murmurs of the air,
> And motions of the forests and the sea,
> And voice of living beings, and woven hymns
> Of night and day, and the deep heart of man. (46-49)

Again, as in the opening lines, is this identification of the poet
with all other physical forms; he is one of the "beloved brotherhood"; his song, too, is as natural, as much a thing of the earth, as
"murmurs of the air" or the "motions of the forests and the sea".

Thus a contrast is established between poet-narrator and poet-
protagonist. Both have been seekers after the secrets of this "unfathomable world". But the poet-protagonist has succeeded in his
search, has searched and gazed and contemplated until

> ... meaning on his vacant mind
> Flashed like strong inspiration, and he saw
> The thrilling secrets of the birth of time. (126-128)

The narrator, however, has given up the attempt to solve nature's
mysteries, is now content to accept his human condition – a condition which prevents him from ever knowing the ultimate secrets.
To him, the world is still "unfathomable". Those critics, and there
are many of them, who see the protagonist as an autobiographical
projection of Shelley himself into the poem, and thus find the
poem full of self-pity, ignore the distinction made between the
narrator, content like Keats with half-knowledge, and the protagonist, who cannot stop until he has solved the riddle of existence.

Furthermore, this distinction sets up a nice contrast between the
narrator's identification with the things of the earth and the protagonist's rejection of the earth. If nothing more can be said, it is
at least obvious that one of them had reached a state in which he
could create poetry while the other remains, so far as we know,
mute and perhaps inglorious.

After this highly significant invocation the narrative begins. The
poem is to be tragic, dealing with the tragedy of a poet who lived,
died, and sang his poems in solitude. Yet his poems had moved
many; strangers had wept and virgins pined and wasted, although

the poet was unaware of them or their sorrow. There follows a detailed description of the poet's life. From early childhood he had intuitively received from nature, from "the vast earth and ambient air", their "choicest impulses". All of "divine philosophy", every-thing good and fine from the sacred past, he "felt and knew". But even then he felt little at home with the rest of humanity: "When early youth had passed, he left/ His cold fireside and alienated home/ To seek strange truths in undiscovered lands" (75-77).

He had searched for these "strange truths" in the most savage and fearful regions of nature; he had pursued Nature's "most secret caves, rugged and dark". In his solitary wanderings, he often lingered in "lonesome vales" where soon the animal life accepted him and would take food from his "innocuous hand". Finally, after his hunger for knowledge takes him to old cities of ancient learning, Athens, Babylon, Egypt, he breaks through the barrier of human ignorance and receives a kind of Faust-like illumination: he understands these "thrilling secrets of the birth of time".

As Gibson has pointed out,

Shelley has thus far described a youth certainly to be admired for his personal attractiveness, his high intellectual pursuits, and his love and sensitiveness to the beauty and wonder of nature.[12]

But, he goes on, the youth had lived a solitary life, "a life un-touched by human love and sympathy". Not that he deliberately refused human companionship; he was simply unaware of its significance or value. We see this in his brief encounter with the Arab maiden who brought his food and worshipped him from afar:

> Enamoured, yet not daring for deep awe
> To speak her love: — she watched his nightly sleep,
> Sleepless herself, to gaze upon his lips
> Parted in slumber, whence the regular breath
> Of innocent dreams arose: then, when red morn
> Made paler the pale moon, to her cold home
> Wildered, and wan, and panting, she returned. (133-139)

[12]   Evan K. Gibson, p. 1027.

This incident, together with the references to the strangers who wept and the virgins who pined to his songs, show "not a deliberate, willful rejection of human companionship but an innocent neglect of a vital part of the human soul".[13]

This neglect is nothing more then, than the "generous error" alluded to in the Preface and, according to Gibson, arose from a highly admirable desire: "the desire to find truth, to find the meaning of life and of the universe. And what heightens the tragedy of the poet's death is the fact that it was caused by an exclusive emphasis upon this very quality which was so commendable in his life." [14]

But, again, let us consider this in the light of the invocation. Was not the search and the successful conclusion to the search as much a part of the "generous error" as the poet's neglect of human companionship?

Although the wanderer loved nature, was enthralled by the beauty of nature, at no time in his wanderings does he ever recognize his own identity as a part of nature. He admires her, but like Thoreau's philosopher, is constantly trying to lift the hem of her gown for a closer look. He is not a part of the natural world; he remains an inquisitive on-looker, not content until the mystery is solved.

His relationship with humanity is only one aspect of his relationship with the natural world. He is not only unaware of the existence of the pining virgin, the weeping strangers, and the passionate Arab maiden, he does not see his own affinity with them. In a word, he denies his own corporeal reality. He is, in fact, the mythical Shelley – the Shelley who, according to some critics, could never acknowledge his own identification with earth, who could never realize that the passion of love is as physically oriented as the movement of the wind in a tree or the flutter of a skylark's wing. And, of course, this fatal flaw in the poet is one that Shelley recognized as exactly that: a fatal flaw. The tragedy of the poem is a direct result of the protagonist's success in piercing the veil

---

13   Evan K. Gibson, p. 1027.
14   Evan K. Gibson, p. 1027.

of mystery. His success as a philosopher-scientist results in his failure as a human being. He is like Oedipus devoting his life to a search for truth, a truth which results in his own destruction.

When, in the Vale of Cashmire, he dreams of the veiled maid, the irony of his situation becomes obvious. Having realized his ambition, having finally broken through the barriers of human ignorance, he has one of the most erotic dreams in the annals of dream literature. I suppose there is considerable psychological validity for this sudden visitation: his chastity, as well as his unbelievable sexual naïveté, would make such an apparition seem like a visitation from another world. But demonstrated here is the awareness Shelley displays of the biological necessity of sexual love. There is nothing here to suggest that this dream-maiden is a Platonic ideal, a mirror image of the poet's own abstracted and distorted consciousness. Of course, the Preface states that the poet "images to himself the Being whom he loves". Furthermore, this image is a combination of intellectual as well as erotic loveliness, a unity of "all of wonderful, or wise, or beautiful, which the poet, the philosopher or the lover could depicture" (Preface). But in the imagery of the poem, the "wonderful" and the "wise" are certainly presented in far less vivid terms than the erotic. Certainly she is a projection from the poet's imagination, but it is an imagination out of control. Until now the "wise" and the "wonderful" had filled the poet's mind. In this projection of "the being whom he loves", another aspect of his nature, that side of him long ignored and denied, becomes predominant. And the poet is ultimately destroyed because of his failure to accept any earthly, physical incarnation of this vision.

The vision of this veiled maid is noteworthy on two accounts: first, the physical, erotic details of her appearance; and second, the progress of the enchantment by which she attracts and seduces the poet, beginning with the intellectual and proceeding to the physical. As he lies sleeping in the Vale of Cashmire,

> A vision on his sleep
> There came, a dream of hopes that never yet
> Had flushed his cheek. He dreamed a veiled maid
> Sate near him, talking in low solemn tones.

Her voice was like the voice of his own soul
Heard in the calm of thought; its music long,
Like woven sounds of streams and breezes, held
His inmost sense suspended in its web
Of many-coloured woof and shifting hues.
Knowledge and truth and virtue were her theme,
And lofty hopes of divine liberty,
Thoughts the most dear to him, and poesy,
Herself a poet... (149-161)

Now this early image of the vision is not particularly sensual. But the maid quite obviously stands for something not within the compass of the poet's experience. She is a "dream of hopes that never yet/ Had flushed his cheek". As we have seen earlier, in his wanderings the poet had ignored everything not directly connected with his search for abstract knowledge. He was hardly aware of the Arab maiden who was sick with love for him; and her rather obvious invitations have had no effect on him. The veiled maiden represents a totally new area of experience.

She speaks to him in "low solemn tones", but at first does not concentrate upon any theme that might offend her chaste victim. We might even suspect a kind of deliberate trap here; such themes as knowledge and truth and liberty and divine poesy are precisely the themes that might allow the unwary poet to take the bait.

But even though no overt sexuality is obvious at first, her voice, which speaks these lofty thoughts, is described in a metaphor composed of sensual terms; it is like "the woven sounds of streams and breezes", suspending his senses in a web. The *web* metaphor is quite appropriate here, for it is a web the maiden spins throughout the enchantment, beginning with her beautiful voice. No matter how lofty the subject matter of her discourse, the sensual music of her voice creates one of the strands that ultimately brings the poet to earth. As the passage continues the maiden's charms are emphasized:

... Soon the solemn mood
Of her pure mind kindled through all her frame
A permeating fire: (161-163)

At this point, the musical metaphor changes from the soft, lulling solemnity of streams and breezes to a primitive, violent music. The maiden breaks into a savage song, accompanying herself on a harp:

> wild numbers then
> She raised, with voice stifled in tremulous sobs
> Subdued by its own pathos: her fair hands
> Were bare alone, sweeping from some strange harp
> Strange symphony, and in their branching veins
> The eloquent blood told an ineffable tale.
> The beating of her heart was heard to fill
> The pauses of her music, and her breath
> Tumultuously accorded with those fits
> Of intermitted song. (163-172)

This fiery performance is described with considerable emphasis upon significantly physical details: bare hands, branching veins, eloquent blood, beating heart, and tumultuous breath. Carried away by the passionate rhythms of her music, the maiden rises, "As if her heart impatiently endured/ Its bursting burden", and reveals her physical charms:

> by the warm light of their own life
> Her glowing limbs beneath the sinuous veil
> Of woven wind, her outspread arms now bare,
> Her dark locks floating in the breath of night,
> Her beamy bending eyes, her parted lips
> Outstretched, and pale, and quivering eagerly. (175-180)

Indeed the erotic description is so vivid that O. W. Campbell protests violently about its appropriateness:

In the passage where Shelley describes the spirit who appears to the poet in a vision and embraces him, there is something hectic, almost offensive: for the description is much too earthly and realistic: she who should have been but a symbol of the soul's desire steps out of the land of Imagery like some scantily dressed beauty of a society ball. . . . Here we have unhealthy sentiment without a doubt, and its very seriousness makes it even more disconcerting than that kind of flippant sensuality so regrettable in Keats.[15]

Following this description is the climax of the entire scene. The

---

[15] O. W. Campbell, pp. 190-191.

love-starved poet, forgetting all thoughts of divine philosophy, gives in completely to this vision of physical loveliness:

> His strong heart sunk and sickened with excess
> Of love. He reared his shuddering limbs and quelled
> His gasping breath, and spread his arms to meet
> Her panting bosom: . . . she drew back a while,
> Then, yielding to the irresistible joy,
> With frantic gesture and short breathless cry
> Folded his frame in her dissolving arms. (181-187)

The entire scene is an obvious image of an erotic dream; the seduction is a physical one, and the rapture of the poet's response to the vision is obviously orgasmic: the maiden responds to the "shuddering limbs" and "gasping breath" of the poet with "frantic gesture" and "short, breathless" cries. A peak of passion is reached, only to fade away with the vision itself at the moment of consummation:

> Now blackness veiled his dizzy eyes, and night
> Involved and swallowed up the vision; sleep,
> Like a dark flood suspended in its course,
> Rolled back its impulse on his vacant brain. (188-191)

As the vision dissipates and dissolves, the poet awakens from the shock of his loss. The very landscape has been transformed from its appearance before the dream. Before falling asleep, he is in a lonely dell "where odorous plants entwine/ Beneath the hollow rocks a natural bower/ Beside a sparkling rivulet" (146-148). But when he awakens, the beautiful spot has changed to one of desolation and emptiness:

> The cold white light of morning, the blue moon
> Low in the west, the clear and garish hills,
> The distinct valley and the vacant woods,
> Spread round him where he stood. (192-196)

Stunned by the disappearance of the vision, the poet questions the universe, and laments the contrast between his present state and his previous joy and exultation:

> . . . Whither have fled
> The hues of heaven that canopied his bower

> Of yesternight? The sounds that soothed his sleep,
> The mystery and the majesty of Earth,
> The joy, the exultation? His wan eyes
> Gaze on the empty scene as vacantly
> As ocean's moon looks on the moon in heaven. (196-202)

All that had occupied his mind before the vision seems meaningless: the vision of the maiden has reduced the previous joy and exultation to nothingness. He is spent and empty, a mere reflection of a reflected light, gazing vacantly upon an empty universe.

The narrative is interrupted now as the reader learns the answer to the poet's questions; we become aware of the specific symbolic importance of the dream. The vision was not a simple projection of the poet's ideals into a human shape as the Preface might indicate. The vision has some substance, aesthetically if not psychologically, outside the poet's own psyche:

> The spirit of sweet human love has sent
> A vision to the sleep of him who spurned
> Her choicest gifts. (203-205)

The dream, then, is a punishment, a means to chastize the poet for his previous spurning of human love. The poet has ignored his own biological nature, his own identity with the "beloved brotherhood". Such an action will lead inevitably to his own destruction.

His dedication to the quest of abstract knowledge, his glorification of reason, becomes a punishable offense rather than a glorious undertaking. The poet's subsequent wandering may be seen as the working out, then, of this theme of vengeance; the veiled maiden is a punitive figure, sent because the poet has spurned the choicest gifts of the "spirit of sweet human love". She is not idealized; she is not "what is perhaps eternal"; she is as physical as a vision can be. She represents sensual love, biological necessity.

The error the poet has made in the past he continues to make after the appearance of the vision. Nowhere does he attempt to find a physical being, a human counterpart of the ideal. Unlike the poet-narrator, the poet-protagonist refuses identification with nature; he fails to understand the significance of his dream. Thus he does not, after the vision, actually seek a human prototype of the

ideal, or any human being at all, a fact which causes R. D. Havens
some consternation in reading the poem:

> He spends his time not in looking for her prototype but in trying to
> stifle the pain of separation and in deciding whether or not death may
> be the doorway to the reunion. Had he really sought her human
> counterpart, he must have associated with his fellowmen, which he
> does not do.[16]

In fact, the poet refused to acknowledge the possibility that a
human prototype exists: She is "lost, lost, forever lost/ In the wide
pathless deserts of dim sleep" (209-210). He has never been aware
of the possibilities of an earth-bound existence; he cannot really
accept the erotic experience of the dream as a reality, based upon
biological fact. He begins his wanderings, not like one in search of
human love, but like one possessed by furies:

> . . . As an eagle grasped
> In folds of the green serpent, feels her breast
> Burn with the poison, and precipitates
> Through night and day, tempest, and calm, and cloud
> Frantic with dizzying anguish, her blind flight
> O'er the wide aery wilderness: thus driven
> By the bright shadow of that lovely dream,
> Beneath the cold glare of the desolate night,
> Through tangled swamps and deep precipitous dells,
> Startling with careless step the moonlight snake,
> He fled . . . (227-237)

The rest of the poem simply works out the punishment, the self-
punishment, of the dedicated poet. There is a kind of inevitability
in everything that follows; he continues to spurn his own nature,
refusing now to even come to terms with his own flesh:

> And now his limbs were lean; his scattered hair
> Sered by the autumn of strange suffering
> Sung dirges in the wind; his listless hand
> Hung like dead bone within its withered skin;
> Life, and the lustre that consumed it, shone
> As in a furnace burning secretly
> From his dark eyes alone. (248-254)

---

[16]   R. D. Havens, "Shelley's *Alastor*", *PMLA*, XLV (1930), p. 1102.

And just as before, he is unaware of the rest of mankind; the human beings he meets in his flight do not exist for him. He is treated with great kindness by the "cottagers/ Who ministered with human charity/ his human wants" (254-256), yet he frightens the mountaineer who encounters him like some strange spirit on the dizzy precipice, and the children who hide their faces from him, "In terror at the glare of those wild eyes,/ To remember their strange light in many a dream/ Of after-times" (264-266). Again the maidens, strangely attracted to this wild-eyed figure, attempt to comfort him, calling him "false names/ Brother, and friend" (268-269), pressing his pallid hand and weeping; but he passes on apparently unaware of their existence.

The conclusion of *Alastor*, describing the poet's allegorical life-journey and his eventual death in solitude, has little specific bearing upon our main purpose here. It is, of course, important in terms of the whole poem, but its primary function is to fill in the details of the poet's untimely death. He dies, as he lived, in solitude.

As the poet-protagonist dies, the narrator laments this death in terms that have often been interpreted as a self-pitying plea for such misunderstood souls, a kind of narcissistic lament based upon Shelley's own feelings about himself. This is ridiculous in many ways. What the last lines of the poem mean is precisely what Shelley indicates in his Preface: that although the poet erred, it was a "generous error"; that the nobility of his efforts is, in some ways, to be admired; that if we must castigate such unfortunates, we should realize that their errors are not so grievous as those who are never deluded by such generous errors:

Among those who attempt to exist without human sympathy, the pure and tender-hearted perish through the intensity and passion of their search after its communities, when the vacancy of their spirit suddenly makes itself felt. All else, selfish, blind, and torpid, are those unforeseeing multitudes who constitute, together with their own, the lasting misery and loneliness of the world. (Preface)

And the final lines of the poem simply restate this basic idea in poetry:

... But thou art fled
Like some frail exhalation; which the dawn
Robes in its golden beams, – ah! thou hast fled!
The brave, the gentle, and the beautiful,
The child of grace and genius. Heartless things
Are done and said i' the world, and many worms
And beasts and men live on, and mighty Earth
From sea and mountain, city and wilderness,
In vesper low or joyous orison,
Lifts still its solemn voice: – but thou art fled –
Thou canst no longer know or love the shapes
Of this phantasmal scene, who have to thee
Been purest ministers, who are, alas!
Now thou art not. Upon those pallid lips
So sweet even in their silence, on those eyes
That image sleep in death, upon that form
Yet safe from the worm's outrage, let no tear
Be shed – not even in thought. (686-703)

This hymn of praise does not excuse the protagonist, does not say
say that he chose the only way to salvation (by denying the world).
He has been destroyed through his own failings. But to a great
extent, so was Hamlet, and so have most tragic heroes been destroyed. And just as Shakespeare makes us aware of Hamlet's
beauty as well as his failures, Shelley tried to do the same with his
central figure. It seems perfectly consistent with a poet's purpose
to divide our responses to some extent, to qualify our sympathies
with insights into the conditions of human nature which make
such quests as the poet's glorious, even if limited by the exigencies
of existence. Shelley is well aware of the limits of the human spirit
in *Alastor*; the poem reveals this limitation and protests that it
should be so. Very little in the poem supports a view that Shelley
is subordinating man's physical being to the spiritual. Perhaps we
can say of it as a whole that it celebrates the attempt to expand
the circle holding in the human spirit, but recognizes, as the hero
does not, that such an expansion must still take place within the
limitations imposed upon us by our own corporeality. As Shelley
stated in the *Discourse on the Ancient Greeks*, without the biological, we are nothing; with only the biological, we are nothing.
Man's sensual nature is admitted, perhaps reluctantly, but none-

theless admitted. And from such admission and recognition, one can progress toward the spiritual; not the anti-sensual, but the more-than sensual.

Epipsychidion, more than any other of Shelley's major poems, seems by its very nature to suggest, even to invite, the idea that Shelleyean love is divorced and abstracted from any involvement with the biological and sensual. Notopoulos finds the poem to be almost "synonymous with Platonism", combining the two strands of Shelley's search for personal sympathy and his quest for Intellectual Beauty; the fusion in Emilia Viviani of "the earthly symbol he had been looking for . . . and the Intellectual Beauty he had been seeking in the world of the mind".[17] Platonic in its very conception, and obviously exploring and trying to define the relationship between ideal and earthly love, the poem has led many commentators to at least partially agree with Woodberry's comments that Emily in the poem is "the general symbolization of the Ideal under the form of woman as in Dante's Beatrice".[18] Ellsworth Barnard insists that "Emilia as a person . . . becomes one more symbol of the Ideal – of beauty and goodness and love – which Shelley sought so persistently. . . . It is no mortal woman whom he would have as his companion on his voyage . . . out of the world of men, to the shores of some island-paradise." [19]

And Carlos Baker, whose commentary upon some sections of the poem is extraordinarily perceptive, finds that the love Shelley is searching for and celebrating in the poem is "as sexless as an angel, for on the spiritual plane where Shelley is standing, sexual distinctions are of no consequence".[20] The presence of the figure of Emilia in the poem and even the consummation described in highly erotic imagery toward the end of the poem, are all to be taken, runs the argument, as pure symbols, as images of that kind of love which is ultimately inexpressible except through a meta-

---

[17] James A. Notopoulos, *The Platonism of Shelley* (Durham, Duke Univesrity Press, 1949), pp. 275-276.
[18] George E. Woodberry, note in *The Complete Poetical Works of Percy Bysshe Shelley* (Boston, Houghton Mifflin, 1901), p. 632.
[19] Ellsworth Barnard, *Shelley's Religion* (Minneapolis, University of Minnesota Press, 1936), pp. 360-361.
[20] Carlos Baker, p. 219.

phor involving sense. Or, as Baker puts it later, metaphorical language was always necessary to express Shelley's conception of love. But this love, "love as goal rather than love as *eros*, often took, so high was Shelley's reverence for womankind, the shape and quality of a woman when he attempted to define it metaphorically".[21]

Anyone who thinks the poem to be a completely literal account of Shelley's real or imaginary affair with a beautiful Italian woman, runs the risk of being classed with those unenlightened souls to whom the poem would be unintelligible. As Shelley notes in the Advertisement, the poem is

sufficiently intelligible to a certain class of readers without a matter-of-fact history of the circumstances to which it relates; and to a certain other class it must ever remain incomprehensible, from a defect of a common organ of perception for the ideas of which it treats.

Now it seems to me both views are over-simplifications, the purely literal view only slightly more so than the purely symbolic view. On the one hand we have the biographical fallacy which treats the poem as a kind of simple transposition of literal fact into poetry. On the other is a different fallacy, the symbolic fallacy we could call it, which refuses to see that the symbol begins in the literal and only after being firmly established there can move beyond the literal. The poem is both literal and symbolic, just as the love celebrated in the poem is both physical *and* ideal, concrete *and* abstract, biological *and* intellectual.

As we have seen, Shelley does not once and for all separate the two aspects of love; he calls for our awareness of the more-than-physical but not, unless we are to meet the fate of the poet in *Alastor*, for the complete abnegation of the physical.

Notopoulos has an interesting observation in this connection where he admits the difference between Shelley's Platonism and Plato's Platonism. In Plato's conception of man's search for ideal Beauty, the actual world is spurned because it is only a symbol, a pale imitation of the ideal. However, Shelley, like Dante, does not

[21]   Carlos Baker, p. 221.

reject or spurn the symbol, but loves it as a poet.[22] The same might be said of Shelley's attitudes toward sensual love. It is inferior because it is not everything; the everything includes the ideal with the sensual. *Epipsychidion* seems to me to be a record of an attempt, in this case a successful attempt, to fuse the ideal with the earthly, not necessarily to transcend the earthly.

As most commentators on the poem have seen, *Epipsychidion* falls into three parts, more or less of equal length: (1) the first part, an invocation to Emily as the image of ideal beauty (1-146); (2) the second part, what Shelley refers to in a letter to Gisborne as the "idealized history of my life and feelings" (147-387); and (3) a third section, the voyage to and the projected life within the Ionian island paradise (388-591). The poem ends with a very brief, but I think significant epilogue.[23]

The invocation to Emily as the symbol of perfection, that ideal beauty which can hardly be comprehended or approached through man's mortal, sensual equipment, suggests that this vision of ideal beauty can never become, in its whole glory, a part of man's experience on earth. Here in the invocation is the vision purified, rarefied, hardly existing except as a gleam or a burning light: "Sweet spirit", "High, spirit-winged Heart", "Sweet Benediction in the eternal curse", "Veiled Glory", "Moon *beyond* the clouds", "Star *above* the storm", "Thou Wonder, thou Beauty, and thou Terror".

She is a harmonizer of all nature, who gives life and meaning, spirit and beauty to the dull world:

> Thou Harmony of Nature's art! Thou Mirror
> In whom, as in the splendour of the Sun,
> All shapes look glorious which thou gazest on! (30-33)

She is one of the highest order of angels, a "Seraph of Heaven", who wears the form of an earthly creature only because in its pure form the vision would be "unsupportable".

---

[22]   James A. Notopoulos, p. 278.
[23]   I have departed somewhat from the traditional division of the poem, feeling that lines 147-189 belong more appropriately to the second section for reasons which I hope will become clear.

> Veiling beneath that radiant form of Woman
> All that is insupportable in thee
> Of light, and love, and immortality! (22-24)

Even this poetry, trying to capture her essence, is a frail vehicle, actually obscuring the vision rather than revealing it. Momentarily the words "flash lightning like, with unaccustomed glow", but they are still "dim words which obscure thee now". The vision is asked to forgive the attempt, poor as it is, to capture her essence in words, but nonetheless to accept it, to smile on it:

> I pray thee that thou blot from this sad song
> All of its much mortality and wrong,
> With those clear drops, which start like sacred dew
> From the twin lights thy sweet soul darkens through,
> Weeping, till sorrow becomes ecstasy:
> Then smile on it, so that it may not die. (35-40)

The poet searches his mind, his imagination trying to find some adequate metaphor, some image to appropriately summarize her qualities:

> . . . Art thou not void of guile,
> A lovely soul formed to be blessed and bless?
> A well of sealed and secret happiness,
> Whose waters like blithe light and music are,
> Vanquishing dissonance and gloom? A Star
> Which moves not in the moving heavens, alone?
> A Smile amid dark frowns? a gentle tone
> Amid rude voices? a beloved light?
> A Solitude, a Refuge, a Delight? (56-64)

But the attempt is fruitless. His "moth-like Muse" burns its wings in the attempt. The narrator finds, after all his effort, only his own infirmity, his own inability as poet to capture the essence of this vision.

Following this failure the poet tries in a different manner to communicate the incommunicable; he describes the effect of the vision upon himself. But after several lines of rather hopeless and abstruse fumbling for metaphors, this new approach falls short:

> She met me, Stranger, upon life's rough way,
> And lured me towards sweet Death; as Night by Day,

> Winter by Spring, or Sorrow by swift Hope,
> Led into light, life, peace ... (72-75)

A new succession of images now begins, and for the first time the metaphors become concrete; the abstract terms drop out:

> ... An antelope,
> In the suspended impulse of its lightness,
> Were less aethereally light: the brightness
> Of her divinest presence trembles through
> Her limbs, as underneath a cloud of dew
> Embodied in the windless heaven of June
> Amid the splendour-winged stars, the Moon
> Burns, inextinguishably beautiful:
> And from her lips, as from a hyacinth full
> Of honey-dew, a liquid murmur drops,
> Killing the sense with passion.... (75-85)

But almost as though rebelling against the lack of ethereality, the poem moves once more into abstract terms of comparison. She is like the "stops/ Of planetary music heard in trance"; finally she becomes "one intense diffusion", "one serene omnipresence" of light and movement.

Then, suddenly, almost as though in a moment of discovery, the angelic symbol is seen as embodied in an earthly form. All of the light, the motion, the spirit, the fire are contained within an earthly vessel, "in that Beauty furled/ Which penetrates and clasps and fills the world" (102-103).

Whereas before, the vision had been insupportable, incomprehensible, veiled "beneath that radiant form of woman", it can now be partially seen: "scarce visible from extreme loveliness", but still " visible".

In the next succession of images, the vision is brought to earth. It becomes quite clear that the symbol of this ideal has become embodied in the real, and the description that follows is of a beautiful, radiant, but nonetheless *real* woman:

> Warm fragrance seems to fall from her light dress
> And her loose hair ...
>
> . . .
> See where she stands! a mortal shape indued

> With love and life and light and deity,
> And motion which may change but cannot die;
>
> . . .
>
> A Metaphor of Spring and Youth and Morning;
> A Vision like incarnate April, warning,
> With smiles and tears, Frost the Anatomy
> Into his summer grave. (105-123)

The invocation has described a kind of progress away from the
infinite down to the finite, from the ideal to the real, which is
purified by the light of the ideal. It begins with the poet reaching,
trying to grasp the white light of the vision, but discovering in the
process the impossibility of doing so. It is not until he sees the
vision in her human, non-spiritual, form, this metaphor or shadow
of the ideal, that she can be contained. The poet realizes that he
has "humanized" the vision, and in the process of making her thus
attainable, may have gone too far:

> . . . Ah woe is me!
> What have I dared? where am I lifted? how
> Shall I descend, and perish not? (123-125)

Could love for this human form make the vision his own? He has
heard that "Love makes all things equal", and could this love for
a human form be the same as a love for the divine? Are the divine
and the human somehow the same? In the next image he expresses
it perfectly:

> The spirit of the worm beneath the sod
> In love and worship blends itself with God! (128-129)

The lowest form of life can, by the ritual of love and worship,
merge with the divine; merger of worm and God is the basic
metaphor for describing the duality of Shelleyan love. Far from a
simple adoration of the ideal, such a relationship accepts the
position of the "worm beneath the sod", rooted in earth, but
suggests the possibility of a union with the more-than-earthly.
There is both a moving up, by the worm, and a moving down by
God. Applied to the whole poem, the metaphor defines the relationship of the poet and Emily. Emily must move down from her
divinity; the poet must seek a way to move up toward the divine.
The possibilities of union are thus suggested in the invocation.

But such a union of the finite and the infinite is, as the poet well knows, impossible under the existing laws, rules, mores, and taboos regulating love. After the invocation has shown that the ideal can be realized in human form, the second section of the poem, including the famous "free-love" passage and the idealized autobiography of the poet, explores the conditions under which such love would have to flourish on earth. As the invocation demonstrates the impossibility of reaching the ideal in abstract terms, the second section shows the conditions which attempt to destroy the ideal on earth.

The section thus begins with line 147, and includes the definition of love, contrasting it with the presently accepted forms of love. The poet's discovery in the invocation has led him now to seriously question the cherished, widely accepted beliefs of the majority of mankind.

> Thy wisdom speaks in me, and bids me dare
> Beacon the rocks on which high hearts are wrecked.
>
> (147-148)

The first obstacle standing in the way of realizing the ideal is the institution of monogomy:

> ... that great sect,
> Whose doctrine is, that each one should select
> Out of the crowd a mistress or a friend,
> And all the rest, though fair and wise, commend
> To cold oblivion, ... (149-153)

Now it does not get us very far to contend, as some critics have, that Shelley does not mean this to be an attack on the institution of marriage, but an attack on something else for which the institution of marriage is only a metaphor of some kind. It seems to me to be a little more specific than Ellsworth Barnard finds it:

One need read into the passage nothing more than a general appeal for the overthrow of jealousy and selfishness, and a special appeal for the treatment of women as persons, as beings possessed of intelligence, capable of friendship, and entitled no less than men to the right to lead their own lives.[24]

---

[24]   Ellsworth Barnard, p. 370.

First of all the poet makes it clear that it is some kind of institution that is under attack. It is a "great sect", with a specific "doctrine", a doctrine which, if adhered to, makes a mockery of love. Here are the conditions now prevailing, conditions which reduce the possibilities of the ideal. Love, instead of a force liberating the human spirit, becomes a means by which man is imprisoned. Lovers become "poor slaves" treading with weary footsteps the beaten road, "chained" to those who might have made them free. We see in this passage, love degenerated from the ideal, love perverted and distorted into its opposite. This "code of modern morals" does not acknowledge the power of love to release and liberate.

Furthermore, this attack on marriage indicates once more that the love being discussed not only here but throughout the poem is sexual. If Shelley were only concerned with ideal love, why should he start his definition of it by attacking an institution whose primary function is to regulate the expression of sexual love in human society? There would be no point in attacking it if it had no particular connection with the ideal that Shelley is trying to establish. He attacks it only because through its control and subsequent perversion of sexual love it destroys the possibilities of an ideal relationship between men and women.

For, the poem continues, man must realize that to control and constrict the free expression of love is to pervert it. True love is not entirely like the elemental things of earth, like gold and clay which diminish as they are used:

> Love is like understanding, that grows bright,
> Gazing on many truths; 'tis like thy light,
> Imagination! which from earth and sky,
> And from the depths of human fantasy,
> As from a thousand prisms and mirrors, fills
> The Universe with glorious beams, and kills
> Error, the worm, with many a sun-like arrow
> Of its reverberated lightning. (162-169)

Restriction upon the expression of love leads only to death of the spirit. Such a narrowing down and focusing on one object destroys rather than conserves.

This expansiveness implies a further characteristic of love: for not only does love expand and flourish in its execution, it is opposed to any restraints at all.

> ... true Love never yet
> Was thus constrained: it overleaps all fence:
> .   .   .
> ... like Heaven's free breath,
> Which he who grasps can hold not. (397-401)

But such a truth about love is generally ignored, if not denied, by most men in the present world. Only a few sages recognize this truth, that "deep well" from which they draw some hope.

The rest of this section of the poem further elaborates and explores the conditions which seem calculated to destroy the possibilities of love. I think we must ignore the approach to the poem which concentrates upon the private, biographical details of Shelley's life for interpretation of this section, identifying the "cold, chaste Moon" as Mary Shelley, the wandering planet as Harriet Westbrook, the sun as Emilia Viviani, and every detail and incident as a thinly disguised account of Shelley's private affairs. The significance of this section of the poem lies, I think, in its analysis of the conditions, described in the preceding lines, which contribute to the failure of love. It develops the theme of the unsuccessful search for love when separated from the ideal vision described in the invocation.

The narrator had once "in the clear golden prime of ... youth's dawn", encountered the Being he now celebrates. But it was a meeting only of spirits in "fairy isles, enchanted mountains ... divine sleep ... wonder-level dreams". The vision at that time, as in the opening lines of the invocation, is totally spiritualized and abstract:

> She met me robed in such exceeding glory,
> That I beheld her not. (199-200)

Far from encountering a real woman, the poet merely intuits the presence of this spirit in the sounds of nature or in objects of art or in the work of "that best philosophy". He realizes that she is that spirit of beauty, like the vision in the *Hymn to Intellectual Beauty*, "an awful shadow of some unseen Power". Her spirit is "the harmony of Truth".

The poet then, like the protagonist in *Alastor*, vows to follow this "lodestar" of his one desire, as a moth attracted by its light might fly toward the evening star, even though it means "a radiant death, a fiery sepulchre". But the moment he begins his search, the vision disappears:

> But She, whom prayers or tears then could not tame,
> Passed, like a God throned on a winged planet,
> Whose burning plumes to tenfold swiftness fan it,
> Into the dreary cone of our life's shade. (225-228)

The poet, like the hero of *Alastor*, will follow her "though the grave between/ Yawned like a gulf whose spectres are unseen". But he hears a voice warning him away from death: a voice which tells him the vision he seeks *is* on earth:

> . . . a voice said: – "O thou of hearts the weakest,
> The phantom is beside thee whom thou seekest. (232-233)

He now begins his search for "one form resembling hers" on earth, a search that seems destined to fail miserably. The account of these failures runs the gamut of possible manifestation of earthly beauty: the treacherous, whose "voice was venomed melody"; the fair whose beauty, being simply earthly, will pass away; the wise, whose "honeyed words betray"; and even the true, but true in a limited way.

Finally, spent and exhausted after his long and fruitless quest, he thinks he finds the mortal embodiment of the vision:

> . . . One stood on my path who seemed
> As like the glorious shape which I had dreamed
> As is the Moon, whose changes ever run
> Into themselves, to the eternal Sun;
> The cold chaste Moon, the Queen of Heaven's bright isles,
> Who makes all beautiful on which she smiles,
> That wandering shrine of soft yet icy flame
> Which ever is transformed, yet still the same,
> And warms not but illumines. (277-285)

Now the striking thing about this extended metaphor of the moon is the emphasis upon its coldness, its frigidity. The moon is "cold, chaste", with "soft, yet icy flames" that illuminate but do not warm. It is also somewhat deceptive, changeable, not really the same as the "eternal sun". It is beautiful; and under its influence, all else is made beautiful. But it is beauty without passion, light without warmth. Its light is not of itself, but reflected; actually, in Platonic terms, it is a kind of imitation of the ideal, not the ideal itself. Under the influence of the moon, the poet (who in terms of the metaphor is the earth) is suspended in a state of passivity, half-way between life and death, lying in a cold, chaste bed. Under her spell, he exists, becoming bright or dim "according as she smiled or frowned on me".

Here is defined an intellectual, idealized, non-physical relationship, far from radiant or fiery or anything else that might identify it with human passion. And following the Tempest and the quenching of the Planet which has exerted a temporary influence upon the earth (poet), the images of death and frigidity describe a relationship that has become even more icy and approximate to the condition of death:

> ... what frost
> Crept o'er those waters, till from coast to coast
> The moving billows of my being fell
> Into a death of ice, immovable. (313-316)

The reappearance of the vision in the poem provides the point of contrast. Compared to the images of the cold, chaste moon, the vision is described in a multitude of sensual, earthly images of sight, sound, and smell:

> Athwart that wintry wilderness of thorns
> Flashed from her motion splendour like the Morn's,
> And from her presence life was radiated
> Through the gray earth and branches bare and dead;
> So that her way was paved, and roofed above
> With flowers as soft as thoughts of budding love;
> . . .
> And odours warm and fresh fell from her hair
> Dissolving the dull cold in the frore air. (321-334)

She is, in contrast to the frigid night, like morning; instead of the ice-like state governed and illuminated by the moon, life radiates from the vision. The gray earth and bare branches are brought to life by her radiance, and thus revived pave her way with flowers, "soft as thoughts of budding love". Her breath is musical, and spreads like light, penetrating into all other sounds, informing and dissolving them. Finally, from her hair come warm, fresh, odors which melt the "dull cold in the frore air".

In contrast to the moon, this being is the bodily, earthly equivalent of the sun, an "Incarnation of the Sun"; hers is the genuine light of love, not the reflected. Like the earth reviving in the spring under the sun's influence, the poet is revived from his long winter's sleep.

> I stood and felt the dawn of my long night
> Was penetrating me with living light. (340-341)

And this "living light" is in contrast to the moon's light which "warms not but illumines".

The movement of this section has reversed the movement of the invocation: moving the poet upward, releasing him from death. The invocation, as we recall, was an attempt by the poet to humanize the spirit; here the spirit returns to etherealize, to lift up the human. And the concluding lines of the second section, an invocation this time to the "Twin Spheres of light who rule this passive earth", attempt to move away from that which is merely earth to an image of an earthly order defined in cosmic terms. Retaining the basic metaphor of the earth-sun-moon, the poet now defines a universe in which these three bodies may function in harmony. The gravitational attraction holding them together is the force of love, free and unrestrained love, as described in the first part of this section. Here is no either/or universe but one united which includes the living light of the vision and the illumination of the moon figure.

> Thou, not disdaining even a borrowed might
> Thou, not eclipsing a remoter light. (362-363)

Thus governed, the earth-poet can exist "through the shadow of the seasons three/ From Spring to Autumn's sere maturity" (364-365).

The harmonious union of the three celestial bodies, which can include even stray planets that may wander into the system, depicts the conditions under which love can become the guiding principle of the human universe. It is to be seen in contrast to the narrow, restricted views held by the mass of men, who adhere to the doctrines of that "great sect", and prepares the way for the last section of the poem which transports this cosmic harmony into its earthly counterpart.

The last section of the poem, then, is not to be seen as an invitation to a flight from the physical world; it is a flight from a physical world dominated by customs, laws, institutions, and sects which constantly interfere and prevent the realization of ideal love in mortal terms. This section departs radically from any concept of a universe split and divided into an immortal world of the ideal and a mortal world of matter. The poem does not suggest flight to a spiritual Elysium, or for that matter to a Dantean Mount of Paradise concealed in the world of the supernatural. The island to which he wishes to fly with the vision is an island on earth, in a definite geographical location: "It is an isle under Ionian skies/ Beautiful *as a wreck* of Paradise" (422-423); it is not even Paradise, but what remains of Paradise on earth.

The poet goes to great lengths to explain its isolated condition: the harbors are not too good. To make it even more specifically a spot of earth, he peoples it with "pastoral people" who are "simple and spirited"; noble savages who from nature itself, "the Elysian, clear and golden air/ draw the last spirit of the age of gold". These people are presumably still innocent through their isolation from the corrupt world described in section two:

> It is a favoured place. Famine or Blight,
> Pestilence, War and Earthquake, never light
> Upon its mountain-peaks, blind vultures, they
> Sail onward far upon their fatal way. (461-464)

This "wreck of Paradise" is a treasure house of nature's beauty, surrounded by the blue Aegean sea:

> There are thick woods where sylvan forms abide;
> And many a fountain, rivulet, and pond,
> As clear as elemental diamond,
> Or serene morning air; . . . (435-438)

The island, though an earthly one, is informed by the breath of the ideal:

> Yet, like a buried lamp, a Soul no less
> Burns in the heart of this delicious isle,
> An atom of th' Eternal, whose own smile
> Unfolds itself, and may be felt, not seen
> O'er the gray rocks, blue waves, and forests green,
> Filling their bare and void interstices. (477-482)

It is a piece of earth, like man; but like man, it has a soul, thus it becomes a physical metaphor to define the position of the lovers toward the ideal. The lovers are encased in bodies; the lady is an incarnation of the ideal; but the love that unites them begins in a geographical location in a mortal cosmos.

To emphasize the naturalness of their projected idyll, a detailed description of the house and grounds in which they will reside is given. It is a man-made dwelling, reared by some mighty "Ocean-King . . . in the world's young prime." But there seems to be nothing to reveal its origin as a "civilized" dwelling. It now seems, like everything else on the island, a part of a free and natural universe:

> It scarce seems now a wreck of human art,
> But, as it were Titanic; in the heart
> Of Earth having assumed its form, then grown
> Out of the mountains, from the living stone. (492-497)

In this earthly Paradise, the lovers will live out their lives, and after death will become like spiritual deities watching over the island:

> Be this our home in life, and when years heap
> Their withered hours, like leaves, on our decay,
> Let us become the overhanging day,
> The living soul of this Elysian Isle,
> Conscious, inseparable, one. (535-539)

But all this will be after death. Meanwhile, still alive and breathing, the poet and his mistress will "rise, and sit, and walk together", wandering in the meadows and climbing the moss-covered mountains in an idyllic relationship, unencumbered by artificial rules of human conduct, within a "calm circumference of bliss".

And in their wanderings they will discover that a kind of sexual activity seems to be the rule of their natural universe: "The blue heavens bend/With lightest winds" to touch the mountains, "their paramour":

> ... the pebble-paven shore
> Under the quick, faint kisses of the sea
> Tumbles and sparkles as with ecstasy —
> Possessing and possessed by all that is
> Within that calm circumference of bliss,
> And by each other, till to love and live
> Be one. (545-551)

Finally, in the concluding lines of this section, the poet and his beloved are united in sexual union, the thought of which leaves him breathless in a combination of ecstasy and despair:

> Our breath shall intermix, our bosoms bound,
> And our veins beat together; and our lips
> With other eloquence than words, eclipse
> The soul that burns between them, and the wells
> Which boil under our being's inmost cells,
> The fountains of our deepest life, shall be
> Confused in Passion's golden purity. (565-571)

Now these lines may, as Baker and others insist, describe simply a metaphorical union. Certainly a union of spirits is taking place in this scene of love's consummation. But a union of bodies is also taking place, a union of bodies and souls. Breath is intermixing; bosoms are bound together; veins are beating in harmony; lips are touching. And the wells which "boil" under our "inmost cells", are mingling in "Passion's golden purity". Certainly if one cannot imagine physical passion being either golden or pure, it is difficult to take these lines straight. But Shelley apparently could imagine physical passion as both golden and pure, especially when such passion involves as well a union with the physical incarnation of the ideal.

This union is as physical and natural and as good as the previous union of mountains and air, or sea and shore is physical, natural, and good. Shelley has described this perfectly in the well-known lyric written in 1819, "Love's Philosophy":

I

The fountains mingle with the river
    And the rivers with the Ocean,
The winds of Heaven mix for ever
    With a sweet emotion;
Nothing in the world is single;
    All things by a law divine
If one spirit meet and mingle,
    Why not I with thine?

II

See the mountains kiss high Heaven
    And the waves clasp one another;
No sister-flower would be forgiven
    If it disdained its brother;
And the sunlight clasps the earth
    And the moonbeams kiss the sea:
What is all this sweet work worth
    If thou kiss not me?

The union of the lovers in *Epipsychidion* is simply another aspect of the natural law of love expressed here.

The movement of section three of *Epipsychidion* can be described then as setting up the conditions under which this culminating union of the ideal and the physical can take place. Only when man can divorce himself from the corrupt world which forces him to separate his spiritual aspirations from physical, can this desired union take place. The island Paradise, separated from the world of men, but intimately associated with the natural world, provides the setting in which this merger of man's divided soul can take place. Here order can be restored in the human cosmos through a free and unrestrained expression of love, based in physical reality but leading to a kind of Keatsian union with essence.

The brief epilogue rounds off the poem, making the poet's escape from the world of men into a world of love a symbolic exodus. This verse, the record of the journey, will go among the chosen few, "that certain class of readers" referred to in the Preface, who can understand, singing that "Love's very pain is sweet,/ But its reward is in the world divine/ Which, if not here, it builds beyond the grave" (596-598).

Far from a heaven divorced from the world then, the blessed isle is an earthly Paradise, a kind of Pantisocratic ideal obtainable through love: a love that is the direct result of the poet's mortal and physical union with an incarnation of the ideal.

Summing up very briefly what seems to be the essential quality of Shelleyan love, we find in Shelley's two major love poems a view remarkably consistent with the views expressed in his prose pieces. As in the *Discourse on the Ancients*, love is more than a simple biological act between savages. But on the other hand, it is not a super-sensuous ideal divorced from the actualities of man's biological being. Although an ideal love divorced from earthly attachments might have seemed to him, as an idea, superior to one based on physical fact, he recognizes, both in *Alastor* and in *Epipsychidion*, the impossibility of ever comprehending or realizing this ideal except in human terms. Certainly there is a kind of ambiguity in his feelings; he would like to believe in the concept of a world of pure spirit: a world divorced from the pains of the flesh. Such a concept is an attractive one, not only to Shelley but to most men who have thought much about it.

The record of Shelley's work indicates an unceasing attempt to make as much as possible of the ideal available in human terms. It does not matter too much whether one applauds or condemns the attempt. But it does matter that we try to see, as clearly as possible, what he actually believed. Perhaps then we can avoid condemning him for his lack of contact with reality or praising him because he celebrates some non-existent celibate paradise. And we must, I feel, realize how fully Shelley is aware of this corporeal basis for man's activities. As Professor Bostetter has put it, a frank recognition of the erotic elements in Shelley's poetry "will do much to make the poetry more acceptable to the modern reader. . . . The greater degree to which Shelley is seen as one who has given expression to an attitude not otherwise defined in poetry rather than as a sentimental Platonist, the more interesting he becomes as an artist." [25]

And for our purposes it is important to see that Shelley ultimately places his faith in the natural world as the only means of knowing divinity or beauty. Although he admired Plato and read him with great sympathy, he differs from the Platonic as well as traditional Christian ethos in that he rejects any superhuman, supernatural hierarchy. The God he seeks is a natural one, enclosed in human flesh and knowable only in human and sensual terms.

[25]   Edward E. Bostetter, p. 213.

IV

KEATS AND THE TRIUMPH OF EROS

It is hardly necessary to document in detail the fact of Keats'
concern with the erotic in his major poetry. We need only recall
the subject matter of such poems as *Endymion, The Eve of St.
Agnes, La Belle Dame Sans Merci*, or *Lamia* to recognize that the
subject was of permanent interest to him. These poems span his
entire period of major productivity, suggesting that the subject
absorbed him not only as a raw youth but even during the relative-
ly mature period of his later work.

Furthermore, the central conflict in each of these poems con-
cerns the claims of a life based upon pursuit of sensual gratification struggling with a sense of dedication to reason and order, or
to the discipline of art. One important critic, Clarence D. Thorpe,
has defined this internal conflict as between "the claims of feeling,
mere intuition or sensation, and those of thought, reason, and
knowledge".[1] Professor Thorpe argues that Keats' entire development as a poet can be seen as an attempt to reconcile this internal
conflict, and he concludes that the forces of reason eventually won
out.

The conflict which Thorpe has outlined certainly exists in Keats'
major work, and a study of these four poems should enable us to
see not only the fact of the conflict, which is obvious to anyone,
but more important, the commentary Keats provides in these
works upon the significances of these forces in conflict. Is it true,

---

[1] Clarence D. Thorpe, *The Mind of John Keats* (New York, Oxford University Press, 1926), p. 32.

as Thorpe suggests and as other commentators have argued [2] that the early poems suggest a pre-occupation with the attractions of the erotic, whereas the last poems indicate a realization that Eros has grave limitations as a figure for worship? Or does Keats' basic attitude toward these conflicting forces remain pretty much unchanged? Is the view of Keats at the end of his brief career, as a mature, level-headed young rationalist who learned the folly of erotic day-dreaming, the philosophical, more "serious" Keats, the correct one? Or is this view an attempt to make Keats' major themes more acceptable to the traditional morality? Let us analyze these poems to see what they, the poems themselves, reveal about the nature and significance of the erotic as treated by Keats.

Keats' first major poem, *Endymion*, although admittedly inferior to his later work, is a good place to start. For the inferiority of the poem has, it seems to me, been admitted too quickly in the past. Nearly every critic has been quick to point out its inadequacies; the poem is crudely executed in places, the rhymes forced, the meter somewhat banal, and even the imagery is often cloying. But if by inferiority one means inferiority of conception – that Keats did not know what he was doing – a close reading of the poem will reveal that it is far from crude in these matters. Most of the poem sticks remarkably close to the central concept; most of the action revolves around a central theme of the quest for erotic fulfillment and the attempt to deify the participants in the quest. Some confusion there undoubtedly is but, as I hope to demonstrate, the poem holds together as a unified and generally coherent structure.

The narrative of the poem describes the quest of the protagonist, Endymion, for the moon-goddess, Cynthia. Book I describes the plight of the hero, smitten by love for the presumably unattainable goddess; Books II and III deal with his quest for the goddess in the underworld and beneath the sea; and Book IV treats the culmination of his quest, the attainment of the goddess,

[2] See particularly Claude L. Finney, *The Evolution of Keats' Poetry* (Cambridge, Mass., Harvard University Press, 1936); Sidney Colvin, *John Keats* (New York, Charles Scribners Sons, 1925); Ernest DeSelincourt, *The Poems of Keats*, edited with an introduction and notes, 6th ed. (London, Methuen & Co., Ltd., 1935), pp. 566-567.

the consummation of his love, and his ultimate deification. The episodes involve such stock mythological figures as Venus and Adonis, Glaucus and Scylla, and others; and in the final book, a rather puzzling Indian maiden appears, diverting the hero from his quest, momentarily at least, through her charms. However, she is later revealed as the moon goddess herself in earthly disguise.

Beneath the literal narrative run several themes, the main one concerned with the power of love to immortalize the lovers. Endymion succeeds in his quest because of his single-minded dedication to the pursuit of love; his devotion to this ideal brings him immortality. His experiences have made him capable of transcending his mortal capacities; as the poem ends he is enthroned with Cynthia in the skies.

Now the poem would present few problems of critical interpretation were it not for Keats' use of the ambiguous word "love", over which a critical controversy of no mean proportions has developed. Does Keats mean that Endymion through intercourse with the goddess has been thus transformed? Or does he mean that through the love of ideal beauty dissociated from the objects of beauty on earth, the hero has reached this blessed state? If he means *sex*, argue some critics, the poem is immoral, silly, and adolescent; if he doesn't mean *sex*, however, the poem is emasculated. Furthermore, a reading of the poem as neo-Platonic allegory must either ignore or distort the obviously erotic imagery of the love scenes.

One of the standard interpretations of the poem is the neo-Platonic one insisted upon by many Keats scholars. In 1880, for example, Miss F. M. Owen interpreted the poem as one in which the main theme is "imagination in all time searching for the spirit of Beauty". Cynthia is the beauty of past ages, and the Indian maiden represents the "new phases on which imagination has entered". Imagination discovers "the eternal unity of all Beauty" and merges with it forever.[3] Very little textual evidence for such an interpretation is presented, and Miss Owen generally ignores the erotica in the poem.

[3] Francis M. Owen, *John Keats: A Study* (London, Kegan, Paul & Co., 1880), p. 85.

But perhaps the best statement of the neo-Platonic interpretation is presented in Sidney Colvin's erudite biography of Keats, the standard biographical study. He argues that *Endymion* deals with "the adventures and experiences of the poetic soul in man".

Keats wrote under the influence of two secondary moral ideas or convictions, inchoate probably in his mind when he began but gaining definiteness as he went on. One was that the soul enamoured of and pursuing Beauty cannot achieve its quest in selfishness and isolation, but to succeed must first be taken out of itself and purified by active sympathy with the lives and suffering of others: the other, that a passion for the manifold separate and individual beauties of things and beings upon earth is in its nature identical with the passion for that transcendental and essential Beauty: hence the various human love-adventures which befall the hero in dreams or in reality, and seem to distract him from his divine quest, are shown to be in truth no infidelities but only attractions exercised by his celestial mistress in disguise.[4]

Elaborations on this theme are continued by a host of critics.[5] What all of these commentators share, is an inability to deal straightforwardly with the eroticism of certain passages in the poem. They either ignore such scenes or deplore them. Colvin, for example, is horrified to discover in the love scene between Cynthia and Endymion in Book II that

their endearments are related, unluckily, in a very cloying and distasteful manner of amatory ejaculation. It was a flaw in Keats' art and a blot on his genius – or perhaps only a consequence of the rawness and ferment of his youth – that thinking nobly as he did of love, yet when he came to relate a love-passage, even one intended as this to be symbolical of ideal things, he could only realize it in terms like these.[6]

---

[4]   Sidney Colvin, p. 171.
[5]   DeSelincourt, Finney, and Thorpe, *op. cit.*; see also Hugh I'Anson Fausset, *Keats: A Study in Development* (London, M. Secker, 1922); John M. Murry, "The Meaning of *Endymion*", *Studies in Keats, New and Old* (London, Oxford University Press, 1939). For an excellent summary of these Platonic interpretations, see Newell F. Ford, "The Meaning of 'Fellowship with Essence' in *Endymion*", *PMLA*, LXII (1947), pp. 1061-1076.
[6]   Sidney Colvin, p. 187.

Such an interpretation could be considered standard until 1947
when Newell F. Ford questioned whether the poem was allegorical in the first place and, if so, whether the Platonic nature of
Endymion's quest was clear from the poem itself. This objection
to the standard interpretation, expanded in 1951 in his study, *The
Prefigurative Imagination of John Keats*, is based upon the belief
that the key to the poem is in the letter to Baily containing the
famous statement: "What the Imagination seizes as beauty must
be truth – whether it existed before or not." Ford argues that the
poem works out Keats' belief in the "pre-figurative imagination",
the concept of the imagination as creative, building from dreams
that which will ultimately become real. *Endymion* is a "fervent
and sanguine testament of young love and its hopeful, prefigurative dreams".[7] The principal theme of *Endymion*, according to
Ford, is the hero's quest of "everlasting fulfillment . . . and immortality of passion".[8] The love of the hero for the Goddess is
neither idealistic nor Platonic in any sense: "the emotional
apogees in *Endymion* . . . are invariably the physical embraces of
the lovers". Keats is simply "celebrating the delights of physical
love", and the moon goddess is "a voluptuous woman bent on
giving and receiving erotic pleasure".[9] The argument of the poem,
continues Ford, is that mortal and physical love guarantees the
immortality of lovers.

A more recent study by E. C. Pettet,[10] seconds Ford's observations and continues the argument against any allegorical interpretation. Pettet sees the poem as a straightforward love poem,
idealizing and glorifying sensuous, physical love. The poem's
sources are in Keats' dreams and unfulfilled erotic impulses. Like
Ford, Pettet calls attention to the erotic elements in the poem and
raises a serious question, one which the Platonizers have generally
ignored: why, if the poem is primarily allegorical, did Keats seem

---

[7]   Newell F. Ford, *The Prefigurative Imagination of John Keats* (Stanford, Stanford University Press, 1951), p. 39.
[8]   *Ibid.*, p. 42.
[9]   *Ibid.*, p. 45.
[10]   E. C. Pettet, *On the Poetry of Keats* (Cambridge, Cambridge University Press, 1957).

so unaware of the allegorical implications? Why, in short, in a Platonic allegory should Keats deal so extensively and in such physical detail with the physical attractions of the goddess? The love ultimately leading to Endymion's immortality is human and sensuous love. This, argues Pettet, is the central statement the poem makes.

The arguments of Pettet and Ford against the poem as allegory, especially Platonic allegory, seem incontrovertible. Not only is there little evidence in Keats' other poetry that Keats ever indulged in Platonic speculation, but the poem itself does not particularly invite an allegorical reading unless we broaden the meaning of allegory to include any narrative with significance or meaning beyond the purely literal.

That Keats had no abstract allegorical concept of the love he was celebrating in Endymion becomes clear when we recall the consternation of his close friend, Baily, a rigid moralist and young clergyman, at the immoral implications of the poem. Writing to Taylor, who was also perturbed by the poem, Baily finds one of the serious faults of the poem to be "the approaching inclination it has to that abominable principle of Shelley! – that sensual love is the principle of things". This principle Baily abhors, quite obviously, calling it a "false, delusive and dangerous conclusion".[11]

Now if Keats had in mind a definition of love other than sensual, certainly he might have pointed this out to the high-minded young clergyman, considering their close relationship while the poem was being written. But apparently no higher moral principle was ever so indicated to Baily by the poet. The point is of minor significance, since we are all aware that a poet's intentions and the finished poem do not necessarily coincide; but the fact is that a feeling existed among the first readers of the poem that it was somewhat immoral. And Keats, so far as we know, never denied such charges.

Actually, only one passage of the poem lends itself to a neo-Platonic reading, the famous "fellowship with essence" passage

---

[11] Quoted by Finney, *Evolution of Keats' Poetry*, p. 321.

(Book I, 777-815), which has been celebrated and discussed far beyond its poetic worth. In these lines, Endymion tries to justify to his sister Peona his pursuit of the dream-maiden by elevating love to the position of highest value in human experience. According to the standard interpretation, this love, this "fellowship with essence", is a kind of Platonic ideal, divorced from the erotic. It is a love of nothing physical says Colvin:

It seems clear that we have . . . shadowed forth the highest hope and craving of the poetic soul, the hope to be wedded in full communion or "fellowship divine . . ." with the spirit of essential Beauty in the world.[12]

And Clarence D. Thorpe defines this love as follows:

Love is the desirable commingling of spirits, the self going out and becoming one with other self. The highest form of union of selves is the union with ideal existence, to be attained through spiritual love.[13]

It seems clear that the word "essence" lends itself to this kind of abstraction and the line "full alchemized and free of space" may be interpreted as some kind of liberation from earthly bonds. But as Ford has shown in his exhaustive study of the passage, Keats' use of the word throughout his poetry and his letters is a rather unusual one: in Keats' writings, "essence" is invariably a synonym for a thing or shape of beauty.[14] Thus, by "fellowship with essence", Keats means not a transcendental union of finite being with the infinite, or any other mystic suggestions: he means "a kind of imaginative 'empathy' with individual, particular, concrete 'things of beauty . . .' essence was a loose name for entities attractive to the aesthetic sense, entities both of the objective world and of the imagination".[15]

Such a reading of this key word puts the passage in an entirely different light: instead of being an invitation to read an allegorical idealization of spiritual love into the poem, Ford's observations

---

[12]   Sidney Colvin, p. 180.
[13]   Clarence D. Thorpe, note to *Complete Poems and Selected Letters of John Keats* (New York, Odyssey Press, 1935), p. 109.
[14]   "Meaning of 'Fellowship with Essence . . .' ", *PMLA*, pp. 1066-1070.
[15]   *Prefigurative Imagination*, p. 15.

force us to recognize the love Keats is elevating in this passage as physical love.

The poem opens with the famous celebration of the things of beauty:

> A thing of beauty is a joy forever:
> Its loveliness increases; it will never
> Pass into nothingness; but still will keep
> A bower quiet for us, and a sleep
> Full of sweet dreams, and health, and quiet breathing.
> Therefore, on every morrow are we wreathing
> A flowery band to bind us to the earth. (I, 1-7) [16]

As Pettet has remarked, these lines do not celebrate beauty in any abstract sense; Keats is apostrophizing the beauty of concrete, objective things, "things" of beauty that will live forever. Here we might well have the key to the poem: a "thing of beauty", restated in line 12 as "some shape of beauty", makes life bearable, even in the midst of depression:

> Spite of despondence, of the inhuman dearth
> Of noble natures, of the gloomy days,
> Of all the unhealthy and o'er-darkened ways
> Made for our searching: yes, in spite of all,
> Some shape of beauty moves away the pall
> From our dark spirits. (I, 8-13)

And these things of beauty, significantly enough, "bind us to the earth", making earth the abiding place of these things and shapes of beauty.

The catalogue of shapes which follows are all concrete and natural phenomena:

> ... the sun, the moon,
> Trees old, and young, sprouting a shady boon
> For simple sheep; and such are daffodils
> With the green world they live in; and clear rills
> That for themselves a cooling covert make
> Gainst the hot season; (I, 13-19)

Later, the "passion poesy" is included in the catalogue, one of the

---

[16] All citations to Keats are to *The Poems of John Keats* (London, Oxford University Press, 1960).

things of earth – things, or essences that "always must be with us or we die".

Now it may be argued that this catalogue and celebration of the things of earth is no answer to the Platonic argument: that the Platonist always and necessarily begins with the beauty of concrete things. But the point is that the Platonist only begins with concrete things: they are the means, if I understand Plato correctly, by which man may progress from love of the sensual to love of the ideal. They are intermediate steps by which man may eventually approach the absolute. But I find it difficult to believe that a Platonist could conceive of these concrete things of earth as "a flowery band to bind us to the earth". Keats is arguing here, not that love of natural beauty is a means to some greater end; as Ford has pointed out, and as the lines of the poem read, the things of the earth are ends in themselves. The worship of nature, in a very Wordsworthean sense, is a means by which the sorrow and pain may be somewhat lightened: the shape of beauty "moves away the pall from our dark spirits".

Following this apostrophe to physical beauty, the narrative proper begins. The scene is set upon the mountain of Latmos and the shepherds of Latmos are celebrating the feast of Pan. Endymion comes upon the scene and is described in images suggesting a fallen god:

> ... His youth was fully blown,
> Showing like Ganymede to manhood grown;
> And, for those simple times, his garments were
> A chieftain king's: beneath his breast, half bare,
> Was hung a silver bugle, and between
> His nervy knees there lay a boar-spear keen.
> A smile was on his countenance; he seemed
> To common lookers on, like one who dream'd
> Of idleness in groves Elysian:
> But there were some who feelingly could scan
> A lurking trouble in his nether lip,
> And see that oftentimes the reins would slip
> Through his forgotten hands: then would they sigh
> And think of yellow leaves, of owlet's cry,
> Of logs piled solemnly. – Ah, well-a-day,
> Why should our young Endymion pine away? (I, 169-184)

This description presents graphically the sad state into which Endymion has fallen: the bugle and boar spear, symbols of the active, martial, and if the boar spear can be seen as a phallic image, the erotic life, are hanging useless. He has no inclination to use either of them.

We do not know at this point the cause for Endymion's distress, but he has lost his effectiveness as a leader. The gloom surrounding him is in sharp contrast with the prevailing atmosphere of joy and celebration. He seems to be dreaming of "idleness in groves Elysian", a hint at the nature of his distraction, but little more than a hint. More important, however, his state is identified, toward the end of the passage, with images of winter, death, and desolation in the minds of his people:

> . . . then would they sigh
> And think of yellow leaves, of owlet's cry,
> Of logs piled solemnly. (I, 181-183)

Not until later do we discover the source of his melancholy. Leaving the festivities, Endymion, at the urging of Peona, his sister, tells of a strange dream. It is beautifully ironic that the realistic, practical-minded Peona believes at first that Endymion has committed some offense against the gods:

> . . . Has thou sinn'd in aught
> Offensive to the heavenly powers? Caught
> A Paphian dove upon a message sent?
> Thy deathful bow against some deer-herd bent,
> Sacred to Dian? Haply, thou has seen
> Her naked limbs among the alder's green;
> And that, alas, is death. (I, 508-514)

Peona, mistress of convention, has the purely conventional habit of mind concerning the relationship of men to their gods. She is somewhat shocked at the idea that he might have caught a passing glimpse of a goddess, and a naked goddess at that! Unable to consider alternate possibilities, she could not suspect the intimate nature of Endymion's relationship with Diana in his dream. She is a fitting representative of the conventional world's attitude toward experience outside the boundaries of the traditional.

Endymion now relates his strange half-dream, half-real experience with the heavenly maiden. The dream, like the poet's dream
in *Alastor*, is an erotic one, and the maiden of the dream is erotical-
ly beautiful:

> . . . locks bright enough to make me mad;
> And they were simply gordian'd up and braided,
> . . . in naked comeliness, unshaded,
> Her pearl round ears, white neck, and orbed brow;
> The which were blended in, I know not how,
> With such a paradise of lips and eyes,
> Blush-tinted cheeks, half smiles, and faintest sighs,
>   . . . her hovering feet
> More bluely vein'd, more soft, more whitely sweet
> Than those of sea-born Venus, when she rose
> From out her cradle shell. (I, 613-623)

The physical details of the maiden's appearance are emphasized
here, far beyond any necessity for a symbol of ideal, non-earthly
beauty.

> . . . As this vision of loveliness
>   . . . like a very maid
> Came blushing, waning, willing and afraid
> And pressed me by the hand. (I, 634-637)

Endymion nearly faints with ecstasy but preserves consciousness
long enough to experience a feeling of floating and plunging
through space with the maiden. Soon they arrive at their destination, vaguely suggested as a den or cavern on a mountain side.
Here the erotic nature of the dream is perfectly defined in
Endymion's distracted behavior:

>   . . . madly did I kiss
> The wooing arms which held me, and did give
> My eyes at once to death: but 'twas to live,
> To take in draughts of life from the gold fount
> Of kind and passionate looks; to count and count
> The moments, by some greedy help that seem'd
> A second self, that each might be redeem'd
> And plunder'd of its load of blessedness.
>   Ah, desperate mortal! I e'en dar'd to press
> Her very cheek against my crowned lip,
> And, at that moment, felt my body dip

Into a warmer air: a moment more,
Our feet were soft in flowers. There was store
Of newest joys upon that alp. Sometimes
A scent of violets, and blossoming limes,
Loiter'd around us: then of honey cells
Made delicate from all white-flowerbells;
And once, above the edges of our nest,
An arch face peep'd, – an Oread as I guessed. (I, 652-670)

It is clear that Endymion has no real awareness of the significance of his dream; he at first believes that yielding to the maiden will mean his death. But he gives in quickly, embracing the goddess even though it may mean giving his "eyes to death". But the exact reverse of death occurs; the embrace of the goddess means life, and Endymion drinks in "draughts of life from the gold fount/ of kind and passionate looks". The erotic vision is superior to all other forms of life: it is something to remember, to store up, to plunder "of its load of blessedness". The word "blessedness" with its religious connotations is a good one here, suggesting the religious nature of the experience: and this suggestion is developed into something like a new religious vision in the rest of the poem.

The dream comes to an end rather abruptly, degenerating into what Endymion refers to as "stupid sleep". But when he awakens, the landscape has been transformed, just as in Shelley's *Alastor* after the vision. The geographical position is still the same; he has apparently not been moved physically from the spot in which he fell asleep. But before his dream, his surroundings had created an atmosphere of serenity and peace; the very sun "unwilling leaves/ so dear a picture of his sovereign power" (O, 547-548).

But as the sun fades from sight,

There blossom'd suddenly a magic bed
Of sacred ditamy, and poppies red:
At which I wondered greatly, knowing well
That but one night had wrought this flowery spell.
(I, 553-556)

These poppies, somehow related to the disappearance of the sun and the daylight, are involved in the dream, for it is their fragrance which brings on Endymion's sleep, preparing him for the vision:

> ... through the dancing poppies stole
> A breeze, most softly lulling to my soul;
> And shaping visions all about my sight
> Of colours, wings, and bursts of spangly light;
> The which became more strange, and strange, and dim...
>
> (I, 566-570)

But after the dream Endymion awakens, and the poppies have been transformed: the scene has changed to one of fearful, melancholy disenchantment.

> ... lo! the poppies hung
> Dew-dabbled on their stalks, the ouzel sung
> A heavy ditty, and the sullen day
> Had chidden herald Hesperus away,
> With leaden looks: the solitary breeze
> Bluster'd, and slept, and its wild self did tease
> With wayward melancholy; and I thought
> ... all the pleasant hues
> Of heaven and earth had faded: deepest shades
> Were deepest dungeons; heaths and sunny glades
> Were full of pestilent light; our taintless rills
> Seem'd sooty, and o'er-spread with upturn'd gills,
> Of dying fish, the vermeil rose had blown
> In frightful scarlet, and its thorns out-grown
> Like spiked aloe. (I, 682-697)

The earth, after the vision, has become a horror house; Endymion, like the poet in *Alastor*, and the knight in *La Belle Dame*, has been left desolate after his experience.

To Peona, however, such a disturbance in the soul of Endymion only indicates a lack of manhood: deriding the idea that any kind of love should create such distressful behavior, she chides him gently, appealing to his pride, his manliness, his sense of duty:

> ... Yet it is strange, and sad, alas!
> That one who through this middle earth should pass
> Most like a sojourning demi-god, and leave
> His name upon the harp-string, should achieve
> No higher bard than simple maidenhood
> Singing alone, and fearfully. (I, 722-727)

She goes on to present what Thorpe refers to as a "practical argument for a life of action as opposed to a life of dreams".[17] Sounding like Pertelot chiding Chanticleer, she insists that dreams should not be considered seriously:

> . . . more slight
> Than the mere nothing that engendered them!
> Then wherefore sully the entrusted gem
> Of high and noble life with thoughts so sick?
> Why pierce high-fronted honour to the quick
> For nothing but a dream?

Peona urges upon her brother a life of action: she calls his attention to the traditional methods of conducting a successful life. She sees his distraction as little more than weakness standing between him and the realization of his full potential as a glorious human being. Such pursuits as Endymion subsequently embarks upon are silly and ridiculous in her eyes, sullying "the entrusted gem of high and noble life" with sick thoughts. Endymion's slack behavior is piercing "high-fronted honour to the quick/ For nothing but a dream" (I, 759-760). It is typical of Peona that she sees nothing in this erotic dream but the possibility of Endymion's eventual dishonor. She cannot comprehend other possibilities of the love experience, and as Endymion quickly points out to her, she dreadfully underrates love in her definition of the "good life".

Endymion's lengthy argument in support of love as the highest possible of human values begins with the "fellowship with essence" passage we have previously discussed. As we have seen, the love Endymion defines here is physical, in no way separated from the sensuous manifestations or "essences" of things. He attacks Peona's previous argument that a life of action is the pinnacle of human achievement.

Endymion admits that previously he, too, had shared this conviction; but he disagrees that his present dream is a purely contemptible one:

> 'Peona! ever have I long'd to slake
> My thirst for the world's praises: nothing base,

¹⁷ Thorpe, *Poems and Letters of Keats*, p. 107.

> No merely slumberous phantasm, could unlace
> The stubborn canvas for my voyage prepar'd ... (I, 769-772)

This dream-experience has raised his hopes for a higher glory. True happiness, he continues, will not be found in the acclaim of the public, but "in that which becks/ Our ready minds to fellowship divine,/ A fellowship with essence" (777-779). It is important to notice here that Endymion is not rejecting the world. He is rejecting the world's praises, the loud voice of public acclaim. He does not make the same mistake as Lycius in *Lamia*, who, as we shall see later, destroys the love-dream by seeking also the world's applause.

Reaching this "fellowship" or identification with essence is a gradual process. We first identify with such natural objects as the rose leaf; then we proceed through sounds, the sound of natural music first – "music's kiss" impregnating "the free winds". This is followed by man-made sounds – songs and old ditties. When we learn to respond to all of this, we have reached a "sort of oneness, and our state/ Is like a floating spirit" (796-797). Finally we reach the ultimate stage, "the chief intensity", the stage of love and friendship. Friendship is a lovely, splendid thing, but makes up the "more ponderous and bulky worth" of human values; for at the very top of this pleasure ladder "there hangs by unseen film, an orbed drop/ Of light, and that is love" (806-807). Love is the ultimate human aspiration.

Following this elevation of love is a long definition of love's influence in human affairs, a passage important enough to quote in its entirety:

> ... It genders a novel sense,
> At which we start and fret; till in the end,
> Melting into its radiance, we blend,
> Mingle, and so become a part of it –
> Nor with aught else can our souls interknit
> So wingedly: when we combine therewith,
> Life's self is nourish'd by its proper pith,
> And we are nurtured like a pelican brood.
> Aye, so delicious is the unsating food,
> That men, who might have tower'd in the van
> Of all the congregated world, to fan

And winnow from the coming step of time
All chaff of custom, wipe away all slime
Left by men-slugs and human serpentry,
Have been content to let occasion die,
Whilst they did sleep in love's elysium.
And truly, I would rather be struck dumb,
Than speak against this ardent listlessness:
For I have ever thought that it might bless
The world with benefits unknowingly;
As does the nightingale, upperched high,
And cloister'd among cool and bunched leaves —
She sings but to her love, nor e'er conceives
How tiptoe Night holds back her dark-grey hood.
Just so may love, although 'tis understood
The mere commingling of passionate breath
Produce more than our searching witnesseth:
What I know not: but who, of men, can tell
That flowers would bloom, or that green fruit would swell
To melting pulp, that fish would have bright mail,
The earth its dower of river, wood, and vale,
The meadow runnels, runnels pebble-stones,
The seed its harvest, or the lute its tones,
Tones ravishment, or ravishment its sweet
If human souls did never kiss and greet? (I, 807-840)

This panegyric is Endymion's justification for abandoning the duties and responsibilities that Peona judges important. None of these public goals can compare in importance with the love quest, Endymion argues; and to further explain his position, he describes those great men who have "been content to let occasion die" and slumber, as he is doing, "in love's elysium". Love thus overshadows even the great public and social accomplishments of mankind. Finally, love is defined as the one great force in the universe, upon which everything on earth is dependent for its very existence: this human, physical love, "the mere commingling of passionate breath", the kissing and greeting of human beings, the orgasmic experience of melting, mingling and combining, is the one great principle of the universe. It is certainly what Baily sees in the poem, "that abominable principle of Shelley! that sensual love is the principle of things".

Having established the principle of sensual love in such a

position of eminence, Endymion now defends his dream as a possible harbinger of good things. He argues that perhaps it was no mere dream; he has seen signs that the dream-experience has some significance beyond mere dreaming. He is beginning to suspect the truth: that the dream may be the means by which the immortal world makes itself known to the mortal. He is not certain of anything, but if his vision does prefigure an ecstatic, sensual love with one of the immortals, no ambition for worldly acclaim can ever come between him and this destiny. This love of the immortal must be the absolute summit of human happiness:

> . . . if this earthly love has power to make
> Men's being mortal, immortal; to shake
> Ambition from their memories, and brim
> Their measure of content: what merest whim
> Seems all this poor endeavour after fame,
> To one, who keeps within his stedfast aim
> A love immortal, an immortal too. (I, 842-849)

Endymion's position is clear. He may be uncertain about the specific steps he must take to obtain the "love immortal", but the traditional pursuits of men seem meaningless and unimportant when compared to this new-found purpose. He dedicates himself to the pursuit of the erotic, and his argument in support of this dedication provides a philosophical justification for his quest.

Book II begins with a further development of the theme; the invocation celebrates the saving powers of human love, declaring the superiority of such love over other forms of human aspiration. "O sovereign power of love", it begins, and continues to describe the recorded histories of human love as the most permanent and significant facts of human history. The purely historical records are dim and shadowy: the siege of Troy, the battles and warfare associated with the siege, all fade "into some backward corner of the brain". But the story of Troilus and Cressida is living, vital, and alive. The vast catalogue of human feats traditionally associated with honor and nobility is rejected: such incidents are of no real concern to human beings:

> Hence, pageant history! hence gilded cheat!
> Swart planet in the universe of deeds!

> Wide sea, that one continuous murmur breeds
> Along the pebbled shore of memory!
> ... What care, though owl did fly
> About the great Athenian admiral's meat!
> What care, though striding Alexander past
> The Indus with the Macedonian numbers?
> Though old Ulysses tortured from his slumbers
> The glutted Cyclops, what care? (II, 14-23)

What is really significant in the life of humanity are the tales of love and lovers:

> ... Juliet leaning
> Amid her window-flowers, – sighing, – weaning
> Tenderly her fancy from its maiden snow,
> Doth more avail than these; the silver flow
> Of Hero's tears, the swoon of Imogen,
> Fair Pastorella in the bandit's den,
> Are things to brood on with more ardency
> Than the death-day of empires. (II, 27-34)

It is the poet's duty to assert the value of love at the expense of the more traditional pursuits of man. As the induction closes, the poet declares his intention to raise "love's standard on the battlements of song". His poem will be a celebration of love, a victory for love over the other forces striving for man's attention and dedication.

The action of Book Two takes place in the bowels of the earth where Endymion has been led by a voice calling from a deep cavern. Pettet argues rather convincingly that this descent into the earth is a kind of symbolic death: that Endymion, having no real hope at this point of ever being reunited with the vision, plunges from "the misery of a seemingly hopeless love" and is tempted to "plunge into the oblivion of death".[18] However, before it is too late, the hero recognizes that death is not the answer to his problems, and prays for deliverance from this predicament in which he has found himself. As Pettet further observes, the early sections of Endymion's adventures underground overflow with images of death, coldness, melancholy. The region he wanders in is "not

---

[18] E. C. Pettet, p. 165.

bright nor sombre wholly,/ But mingled up; a gleaming melancholy;/ A dusky empire . . ." (II, 222-224). Endymion feels himself growing "chilly and numb" and when he finally stops his aimless wanderings through the labyrinthine underground corridors, he realizes he has been led here by a kind of self-deception. "The journey homeward to habitual self" (II, 276).

The scene begins to change as soon as he prays to Diana: the cold marble floor is transformed to "leaves . . . and flowers, and wreaths, and ready myrtle crowns" (II, 341-'42). He is apparently symbolically released from the death to which he had previously consigned himself. Immediately following this release, Endymion witnesses the annual reawakening of Adonis, as the Venus-Adonis myth is acted out before him. It requires no great imaginative leap to see the relevance of this myth to the theme of Keats' poem. This myth is an archetype of the vegetation myth. The rebirth of nature in the spring from the death and desolation of winter is suggested by and associated with the story. The rebirth of the earth is intimately bound up with the erotic love-making of the two figures in the myth. It is a kind of mythic commentary upon the question Endymion has asked in his own philosophical musings in Book I:

> . . . Who, of men, can tell
> That flowers would bloom, or that green fruit would swell
> To melting pulp, that fish would have bright mail,
> The earth its dower of river, wood, and vale,
> The meadows runnels, runnels pebble-stones,
> The seed its harvest, or the lute its tones,
> Tones ravishment, or ravishment its sweet
> If human souls did never kiss and greet? (I, 835-842)

The answer is given here in the re-enactment of the myth; erotic love *is* the principle of all things.

It seems significant that immediately after viewing the mythic scene, Endymion is blessed by Venus who offers him hope of eventually succeeding in his quest. The blessing is followed by a brief appearance of the moon goddess and the two lovers are united for a brief but passionate love scene. This scene is undoubtedly the climax of Book II, the point toward which the action has been leading. Until now, Endymion's only contact with the goddess has been in the form of a somewhat ambiguous vision: ambiguous because Endymion was not certain whether the encounter had been real or dream. But now the goddess comes to him in person; the physical contact with her convinces Endymion of what he had previously only suspected; that the dream was real.

> Stretching his indolent arms, he took, O Bliss!
> A naked waist: 'Fair Cupid, whence is this?'
> A well known voice sigh'd, 'Sweetest, here am I!'
> At which soft ravishment, with doting cry
> They trembled to each other. (II, 712-716)
> Long time in silence did their anxious fears
> Question that thus it was; long time they lay
> Fondling and kissing every doubt away;
> Long time ere soft caressing sobs began
> To mellow into words, and then there ran
> Two bubbling springs of talk from their sweet lips.
>   (II, 733-738)

Pettet finds this love scene a great disappointment. He calls it "probably the worst passage in the poem; it is a piece of unabashed eroticism, vulgar and sickly-sentimental by turns".[19] Now his charge of sentimentality is no doubt justified: the lovers' conversation, particularly their parting remarks, is sentimental tripe. That the passage is erotic is also true. But what else could it have been? Keats is apparently trying to make it clear that the love-making between the couple is physical intercourse. Judging from some of the readings of the poem, the passage may not have been quite erotic enough. But erotic, vulgar, or whatever else one wishes to call it, the scene is undoubtedly the climactic moment of the second book, the dramatic statement of the theme introduced in the induction and in Endymion's eulogy to love in Book I.

Cynthia promises Endymion that his devotion to the love quest, if steadfast, will lead him to a state of blessedness; through a kiss he will be transformed, immortalized:

> . . . Now a soft kiss —
> By that kiss, I vow an endless bliss,

19   *Ibid.*, p. 171.

> An immortality of passion's thine:
> Ere long I will exalt thee to the shine
> Of heaven ambrosial; and we will shade
> Ourselves whole summers by a river glade.
>   (II, 806-811)

Cynthia's heaven, we see, is a place where refinements on mortal love are continued for an eternity; it is a lover's paradise of eternal passion:

> My happy love will overwing all bounds!
> O let me melt into thee; let the sounds
> Of our close voices marry at their birth;
> Let us entwine hoveringly. (II, 814-817)

The "happy love" here, unlike the happy love of the *Ode on a Grecian Urn*, is a love ending in consummation rather than expectation indefinitely prolonged. But in both poems there is little doubt that the love refers to erotic impulses, whether satisfied or simply aroused.

Because Endymion is not quite ready yet for immortality, and since Cynthia must prepare the other gods for the paradox of the goddess of chastity taking a lover, and of course because Keats still has 2000 more lines of poetry to attain his stated goal, the poem continues for two more books. But the central motif of the poem has been powerfully emphasized and developed by the end of Book II.

Book III is primarily a narrative of transition; here, through his adventure under the sea, Endymion seems to prepare himself for his final triumph in the last book. He seems to have succeeded in his quest but before his final consummation he must perform one task, a task which seems to have been prepared for him far back in antiquity and the successful completion of which will prove him to be a kind of love's messiah, the savior of those lovers who through their constancy to love are worthy of salvation. The action of Book III resolves around this single significant act, the resurrection of the lovers.

As he wanders alone with "the giant sea above his head", Endymion comes upon the old man of the sea, Glaucus, who has been waiting for the appearance of the man who, it had been prophesied, would perform this task of liberation from death. As Glaucus sees Endymion approaching, he awakens as from a trance, "like one whose tedious toil/ Had watch'd for years in forlorn hermitage", (III, 226-227) and proclaims him to be the deliverer:

> 'Thou art the man!' Now shall I lay my head
> In peace upon my watery pillow: now
> Sleep will come smoothly to my weary brow.
> O Jove! I shall be young again, be young! (III, 234-237)

Glaucus continues his oration of rapture, an extended song of joy that the young mortal's appearance has released him from his vigil and from the pains of age, "this serpent-skin of woe". He ends with the repetition of his cry of recognition, "Thou art the Man!" Later, he explains to Endymion, who suspects for a moment that the old man is prophesying some horrible fate awaiting him, that he had been long expected and that he is, in fact, the savior for whom this world had been waiting in gloom and weariness.

> . . . thou openest
> The prison gates that have so long opprest
> My weary watching. Though thou know'st it not,
> Thou art commission'd to this fated spot
> For great enfranchisement. (III, 295-299)

Furthermore, Glaucus continues, he, Endymion, had been cast in this role because of his love for Cynthia.

> . . . hads't thou never lov'd an unknown power
> I had been grieving at this joyous hour. (III, 301-302)

The religious overtones of this scene are striking. Endymion, quite obviously, is being identified as a Savior here, but a Savior who will redeem the world through physical love rather than spiritual. Endymion's devotion to this erotic quest makes him the proper figure to become, as we shall see in Book IV, a romantic version of the man-god.

The remainder of Book III is taken up with Endymion's actions as redeemer; Glaucus leads him to the caverns where the dead lovers lie awaiting his coming. Following the instructions of Glaucus, Endymion scatters the torn pieces of the old man's scroll upon the dead lovers and they awaken, rejoicing in their victory over Death.

The happy reunited lovers rush away to celebrate at Neptune's palace, and there Endymion falls asleep again; but his task has now been performed and in his sleep he hears the words of his beloved goddess, congratulating him upon his act prophesying their forthcoming happiness:

> Dearest Endymion! my entire love!
> How have I dwelt in fear of fate: 'tis done –
> Immortal bliss for me too hast thou won.
> Arise then! for the hen-dove shall not hatch
> Her ready eggs, before I'll kissing snatch
> Thee into endless heaven. Awake! Awake!
>
> (III, 1022-1027)

Thus Endymion through constancy to the erotic goddess has shown himself worthy to be immortalized; and it is a vindication of Endymion's argument in Book I that dedication to love leads to usefulness greater than that of a practical man of action. The final book of the poem is concerned with the process of immortalization and the means by which it will take place.

It is somewhat surprising to discover that the steadfast Endymion, dedicated to the pursuit of the immortal goddess, seems on the verge of failure in the final book. Having successfully pursued his ideal through three books, having come unscathed through the horrors of the underworld, the dangers of the ocean and even the chidings of the puritanical Peona, he suddenly seems on the verge of wavering from his quest when a beautiful and mysterious Indian maiden appears from nowhere and apparently divides his loyalties. As Book IV begins, Endymion hears a plaintive voice, sorrowfully lamenting the loss of home and friends. He investigates the source of this voice and discovers the maiden whose breathtaking beauty strikes him dumb. He suddenly discovers himself torn between loyalty and love for Cynthia and this spontaneous, uncontrollable desire for the beautiful maiden. The conflict renders him utterly wretched:

> ... Upon a bough
> He leant, wretched. He surely cannot now

Thirst for another love: O impious,
That he can ever dream upon it thus! (IV, 86-89)

But even though his fidelity to his love quest had led him through "the dark earth and through the wondrous sea", and although he proclaims to the goddess, "I love thee not the less: from thee/ By Juno's smile I turn not – no, no, no –" (IV, 92-93) nonetheless he cannot resist the earthly charm of this beautiful Indian. He agonizes: "For both, for both, my love is so immense/ I feel my heart is cut for them in twain" (IV, 96-97).

This agonizing conflict continues for the rest of the poem. On a mysterious journey into the sky with the maiden, he is alternately attracted to the beauty of the goddess when she appears and the beauty of the mortal maiden by his side. But when the goddess fades away, he feels as passionately as ever about the creature of earth. When Cynthia reappears and the maiden fades away, he is overcome with consternation, and when he discovers the maiden again he is fired with love for her warm reality. He gives up his dream, his quest, the goddess, and decides to live on earth with the maiden and never more dream of immortal love or union with the gods. But then the maid refuses him, reluctantly insisting that she is forbidden to yield to him. Finally, after the bewildered and confused youth in a paroxysm of passionate rejection of everything – Cynthia, Indian maiden, and all – vows to live alone in a cave, Cynthia appears again and resolves his dilemma by revealing that she and the Indian maiden were the same figure all the time. Cynthia merges into the Indian maiden and the two lovers are enthroned in the heavens, fulfilling the prophecy of Book II. The poem closes as Cynthia vows that she and Endymion will henceforth roam and bless the forests of Latmos; and the happy pair fade away.

Now much of the action of the last book is confusing, and this confusion has led to some rather confused discussions over its significance and meaning. The Platonists' answer is provided by what I feel is their misinterpretation of the preceding books. If Cynthia represents ideal beauty, they argue, Keats must be asserting here that this ideal beauty can only be achieved through human love. The Indian maiden is the earthly manifestation of this ideal, other-worldly, spiritual essense of beauty with whom Endymion has been having a purely idealized and non-erotic relationship. But, of course, as we have seen, Endymion seems to have been having an erotic, if erratic, relationship with the goddess long before the Indian maiden appeared, which seems puzzling. And Pettet, rejecting this interpretation, as I do, argues that Keats was only a boy of twenty when *Endymion* was written, and the last book shows us his youthful conflict between his desire for real, earthly, physical love and his poetic aspirations. Here Pettet unwittingly allegorizes the moon goddess again, making her into the symbol for poetry. What Endymion has been doing making love to poetry is not clear, but as Pettet insists, this same conflict occurs in *La Belle Dame* and *Lamia*. At the age of twenty, Keats could apparently still indulge in "the fancy that the dream-goddess and human maid are actually one – which is, of course, what we should all like to believe at one stage".[20]

It does seem to me that we can read the final book of *Endymion* as a rather fitting conclusion to all that has taken place in the first three; Book IV is simply a unifying development of the deification of erotic impulses which we have seen throughout the poem. Keats is trying to make it indisputably clear that erotic love is the supreme value. He does this by suggesting that love for an immortal goddess and love for a mortal woman are the same. Keats is ending the poem on the same idea he has developed throughout, showing the almost supernatural power of human love to immortalize those who worship at its shrine.

The introduction of the Indian maiden into the poem is necessary and structurally in keeping with everything else of importance in the poem. Had Endymion finally achieved his quest, had he in the final book, through some mysterious cosmic process, been simply immortalized through his uncontaminated, unswerving fealty to the moon goddess, the poem would have to be read as an imaginative dream-phantasy. But Keats knows that the traditional connotations of goddesses are not the same as for mortal woman; and a poem in which human love is symbolized only through an encounter between an immortal and a mortal might imply a far more unearthly quality in the love than Keats wishes to allow. Thus the love of the immortal, which has sustained Endymion throughout his love-quest, must be shown as other than a spiritual, idealized non-physical love. The introduction of the Indian maiden emphasizes this important point.

The seeming paradox of the fourth book centers in the apparent momentary swerving of Endymion from his devotion to the goddess. Both Endymion and the reader are led to believe that the wavering exhibited here, the reversals of feeling from passionate love for the earth maiden to dedication to the object of his quest, reveal a confusion, perhaps even a falling away from his devotion to Cynthia. But actually Keats seems to be suggesting that the quest for love is not a quest for the ethereal and the spiritual. It is not a Platonic, non-sexual immortality that Endymion seeks, but an "eternity of passion". He must discover some object of that passion in earthly guise, a "*thing* of beauty" which is seen in purely earthly form and loved for its earthly form. Furthermore, there is even a suggestion here of something like a Blakean dedication to physical love itself, rather than some particular code of constancy to a specific object. Endymion is dedicated to love in whatever guise it appears. As we have seen, he loved the Indian maiden and Cynthia, both equally: "For both, for both, my love is so immense/ I feel my heart is cut for them in twain." The actions of Endymion in Book IV resemble the narrator's outbreak in Shelley's *Epipsychidion* against the custom of monogomy which proscribes constancy to one object at the expense of love itself.

Thus, because Endymion loves both equally, he becomes pure enough in the service of love to obtain both. His love for the maiden is a part of the same passionate love in pursuit of which he had devoted his live. At the end of the poem, when Cynthia reveals to him that she is both mortal and divine, goddess and woman, the two kinds of love are seen as identical. We have a mingling of the divine with the human; the divine becomes human and the human becomes divine. The transformation takes place not through remote search through the realms of abstract philosophy or speculation; man achieves god through a dedicated quest

for woman. Through the exploration of the senses, through physical earthly love, man becomes his own divinity. The divinity is a
part of man, and the becoming takes place within the sphere of
human activities.

Endymion learns, through his attachment to the Indian maiden,
that he is powerless to transform his earth-bound emotions into
ethereal, abstract feeling. Insofar as such emotions are a part of
man's physical makeup, their full fruition depends upon directing
them toward a physical object.

Thus we can see that the action at the end of the poem, the
deification of Endymion, has been qualified by the previous
humanization of Cynthia. The action is a dual one: through
humanizing the goddess, Endymion is immortalized; and in order
to immortalize Endymion, Cynthia must be humanized. Their
future existence is even a qualified one: they will not reside in the
skies or on Mt. Olympus with the other deities, dissociated from
earth. For as Cynthia informs Peona, just before the lovers depart,

> . . . Peona, we shall range
> These forests, and to thee they safe shall be
> As was your cradle; hither shalt thou flee
> To meet us many a time. (IV, 995-998)

Their realm shall be the earth, just as the love which makes their
union possible is an earthly one.

The poem, as we have said before, is a love-quest poem; the
protagonist is motivated throughout by a totally uncontaminated
devotion to the erotic impulse. Through his devotion to this impulse, he is deified. Man becomes god through exploration, search,
and discovery of that which the impulse drives us towards, the
erotic object. And we discover basically the same theme at work
in Porphyro's quest in *The Eve of St. Agnes.*

Critics are nearly unanimous in agreement that the major
theme of *The Eve of St. Agnes* is a celebration of human love.
Although a few, notably Sidney Colvin and de Selincourt, protest
the essential purity of the scene in Madeline's bed, even those who
have contributed to the allegorization of Endymion seem to realize
that here at least the love between Porphyro and Madeline reaches

a physical consummation and the poem celebrates this consummation as one of man's most valuable and ennobling experiences. As Middleton Murry sums up the theme of the poem:

> ... We may fairly call it a poem of opulent and triumphant love. It has the rapture and enchantment, the rich and deep and right sensuousness, of complete surrender to the god; it is the brief dayspring of Keats's passion translated into terms of poetic imagination.[21]

And E. C. Pettet, generally in agreement, calls it "a great affirmation of love – of an intense, happy, achieved love . . ." [22]

In short, there is little controversy over the main theme of the poem; and for our purposes it is a perfect expression of Keats' tendency to deify the erotic – to supplant the old gods of reason and self-denial with the new gods of human love and self-exploration. Like *Endymion, St. Agnes* establishes a religious motif centered around the ideal of consummated human passion. It rejects the traditional, reason-oriented, publicly motivated world of social forces, a world symbolized in the poem by the Beadsman – representative of the institutionalized, traditional, God-centered world – and the brawling, drinking, fiercely war-like and protective members of Madeline's family. These representatives of the real, historical world are related to those in *Endymion*, those who participate in the vast pageant of human history rather than the pageant of human love: figures who are banished into "some backward corner of the mind" in order to celebrate instead the stories of lovers.

The first line of the poem strikes the contrast between these two orders: "St. Agnes' Eve – Ah bitter chill it was." On the one hand we have the legend connected with the Eve of St. Agnes that

> Young virgins might have visions of delight
> And soft adoring from their loves receive
> Upon the honey'd middle of the night
> If ceremonies due they did aright. (47-50)

---

[21]   John M. Murry, *Keats and Shakespeare* (London, Oxford University Press, 1925), p. 109.
[22]   E. C. Pettet, p. 212.

Opposed to the legend is the chill of the actual night, disconnected from the legend.

The first stanza introduces the Beadsman with his numb fingers and "frosted breath/ Like pious incense from a censer old", who is identified with the chill night rather than the "warm" legend. Here in the chapel, surrounded by the statues of the dead, the "sculptored dead . . . imprisoned in black purgatorial rails", the Beadsman will pass the night, "among rough ashes" . . . for his soul's reprieve, grieving for the sins of the world. This figure of the chill Beadsman, praying in the chapel, remains in thematic counterpoint throughout the poem. His "harsh penance on St. Agnes' Eve" is in vivid contrast with the love-making of Porphyro and Madeline. Both he and the lovers seek salvation, but only the lovers are saved.

The setting for the Beadsman's lonely vigil is an appropriate one – in a chapel which serves as a family tomb. Engaged in the traditional, pious, self-denying worship before the "sweet Virgin's *picture*", he is also identified with the statues of the sculptured dead surrounding him. He symbolizes not only the religious order, but the close identification of traditional religion with the feudal society. The tomb and the family chapel are the same; this place of worship is a place of death. The Beadsman's asceticism is a worship of death, for "already had *his* deathbell rung".

The noise of the festivities in the castle reaches the Beadsman surrounded by the stone symbols of the fate awaiting the celebrants; and as they celebrate the festival, they are watched by stone angels:

> The carved angels ever eager eyed,
> Star'd, where upon their heads the cornice rests,
> With hair blown back and wings put cross-wise on their breasts.
>
> (34-36)

Nearly every detail in the first four and a half stanzas seems designed to emphasize first of all the death-like chill engulfing nature and the Beadsman and permeating the holiday atmosphere of the crowd. The celebrants are like unconscious participants in a dance of death, glittering in their plumes, tiaras, and rich clothing, but closely and inextricably connected to the scene in the chapel with the aging Beadsman among the tombs and ashes.

But accompanying the scenes of chill and death associated with the traditional religious observances, whether in the chapel or the hall, is the possibility of a different kind of worship. St. Agnes' Eve suggests not only fasting, praying, and riotous celebration in the midst of death; it also suggests dreams of love, dreams of erotic fulfillment, dreams of warm and passionate living relationships between men and women. And it is quite significant that the poem deliberately turns away from the former ritual and fastens our attention in stanza five upon Madeline, "whose heart had brooded all that wintry day/ On love, and winged St. Agnes' saintly care" (43-44).

Her thoughts focused upon the legend of love associated with the holy day, Madeline is oblivious to her surroundings, unaware of the music "yearning like a God in pain", as well as the "amorous" cavaliers who attempt to engage her attention but are not even seen. She is obviously not a part of this aspect of the ritual; and we are being prepared for the erotic adventure in her bed chamber which will ultimately lead to her release from it. During the entire festival her thoughts have been centered on her bed where the erotic fulfillment of her "Agnes' dreams, the sweetest of the year", awaits her.

Accompanying this erotic-religious theme is Porphyro's worship of love and the immediate object of love, the maiden Madeline. While the inhabitants of the castle celebrate the old ritual, Porphyro waits outside the walls observing a ritual of his own, praying like the Beadsman, but praying to the saints for the satisfaction of his own passionate desires:

> . . . Beside the portal doors,
> . . . stands he, and implores
> All saints to give him sight of Madeline,
> But for one moment in the tedious hours,
> That he might gaze and worship all unseen;
> Perchance speak, kneel, touch, kiss –
> in sooth such things have been. (76-81)

Madeline is a kind of religious symbol to Porphyro, a symbol, like the other virgin, of worship; but the worship is far less spiritual. Porphyro, like a religious communicant before a holy shrine, prays for a miracle – but a profane miracle: he desires not spiritual salvation but erotic consummation. This religious-symbolic identification of Madeline continues throughout the poem. Later, as Porphyro concealed in her room watches her at prayer, she is described in explicit religious imagery:

> Rose-bloom fell on her hands, together prest,
> And on her silver cross soft amethyst,
> And on her hair a glory like a saint:
> She seem'd a splendid angel, newly dress't,
> Save wings for heaven. (220-224)

And the image continues, shifting to that of a pagan goddess emerging from the sea, as the naked Madeline is described with her gown at her feet:

> Half-hidden like a mermaid in sea-weed,

As Porphyro prepares the feast for the sleeping Madeline, his actions suggest the preparation of a shrine. The table is covered with "a cloth of woven crimson, gold and jet", and the food, all the delicacies the rich earth provides for the palate, includes "manna", the food of the gods.

As he tries to awaken the maiden, Porphyro makes explicit what the imagery has up until now only been suggesting:

> And now, my love, my seraph fair, awake!
> Thou art my heaven, and I thine eremite. (276-277)

The shrine is complete, the goddess invoked, and all that remains is the successful attainment of the quest:

> Beyond a mortal man impassioned far
> At these voluptuous accents, he arose,
> Ethereal, flush'd and like a throbbing star
> Seen mid the saphire heaven's deep repose:
> Into her dream he melted, as the rose
> Blendeth its odour with the violet, –
> Solution sweet: meantime the frost-wind blows
> Like Love's alarum pattering the sharp sleet
> Against the window panes; St. Agnes' moon has set.
> (316-324)

Through physical consummation with the erotic object of his quest, Porphyro has, like Endymion, been immortalized – he is more than mortal, identified now with the timeless and eternal star in "heaven's deep repose".

We have been brought from the first scenes dominated by images of cold and death, with warm and throbbing life only implicit in the legend, to the scene with the lovers in bed, in each other's arms, the wind and sleet outside pattering the window panes. The legend has become fact. Reality is outside the fact. What had been suggested, what had been consistently identified with the dream, is now real. And Porphyro assures Madeline of this: "This is no dream, my bride, my Madeline!"

Before stealing away from this house of death, Porphyro declares his eternal fealty to his goddess, once more defining his relationship to her in religious terminology:

> Ah Silver shrine, here will I take my rest
> After so many hours of toil and quest,
> A famish'd pilgrim, – sav'd by miracle. (337-339)

As Keats himself, several months later in a letter to Fanny Brawne, has stated, "I could be martyr'd for my Religion – Love is my religion – I could die for that." [23]

Thus we have in the poem essentially the same theme we have discovered in *Endymion*, and this time there is little doubt that the love being celebrated is sensual. Love has become the principle of life, a force worthy of worship. The traditional rituals of worship lead only to death. The forces of society, identified with the religion of death, are antagonistic to this erotic impulse, but they fail to stop its free expression here. As the lovers creep through the halls toward freedom, the inhabitants of the castle sleep fitfully in drunken slumber; the passage is fraught with danger, for they are like "sleeping dragons all around,/ At glaring watch, perhaps with ready spears –".

This is the world, we will discover, that succeeds in *La Belle Dame Sans Merci*, in bringing the knight-at-arms away from the immortal, warm and passionate world of the "elfin grot" and deposits him "alone and palely loitering" on the cold hillside. But Madeline and Porphyro, like Endymion and Cynthia, triumph over this world of knights and warriors. Their home in the southern moors awaits them; theirs is a paradise based on the worship and exaltation of the flesh. The world they leave is the inferno where the Baron dreams "of many a woe" and "all his warrior guests with shade and form/ Of Witch and demon, and large coffin worm,/ Were long benightmared".

Even old Angela, the helpful duenna, cannot escape this world, love being denied her even though she may be love's willing accomplice. And the Beadsman, the seeker of eternal life through privation and penance, "after thousand aves told,/ For aye unsought for slept among his ashes cold" (377-378).

V

KEATS AND THE FAILURE OF EROS

Traditional interpretation of Keats's works usually describes the development of the poet in terms of some kind of progression toward a somewhat moral and intellectual plane. The early *Endymion* is a love phantasy in which Keats's impulses in the direction of the erotic are sublimated under a cloak of allegory; *Eve of St. Agnes* is another poem of the same nature, but one in which the erotic is frankly glorified. But somewhere between the completion of *St. Agnes* and the composition of *La Belle Dame Sans Merci*, the young poet miraculously matured. For according to this argument, in *La Belle Dame*, Keats began to see the error of his ways. He began to realize that his youthful dreams of "eternities of passion", his earlier celebrations of the flesh and love's fulfillment, were childish fancies. His difficulties with Fanny Brawne, the complications of his life as he tried to reconcile the claims of his passion for Fanny with the demands made upon him by his art, his financial and economic woes which kept him from marriage and the fulfillment of his erotic dreams – all of these troubles combined, forcing him to see squarely and realistically the inadequacies of Eros.

Thus, the argument runs, *La Belle Dame* presents love, or the symbolic figure of love, the beautiful lady of the meads, as a cruel destroyer. Keats, in the space of roughly two months, the time between *St. Agnes* and *La Belle Dame*, changes from a passionate celebrant of love's victory to a cynical observer of love's destructive effects. This attitude toward love is to prevail throughout the rest of Keats' brief creative life, and reaches its climax in *Lamia*. Both of these later poems reveal a more "mature" Keats, a poet who had progressed to an intellectual awareness that love can destroy as well as create.

Even the more recent studies of Keats tend to adopt a similar view of the poet's development. In a study published in 1959, for example, Bernard Blackstone comments upon this change. According to Mr. Blackstone, *Endymion* is the key poem to an understanding of Keats. He calls it "the great expansive, the great embracing poem",[1] in which all the great themes of his later work are struck for the first time. *Endymion* deals primarily, he admits, with the theme of sexual love: this is the "imperial theme". This theme is taken up in at least four of Keats' major poems and each of these poems deals with a different aspect of love.

... All these offshoots from the great forest tree of *Endymion* are luxuriant or stunted expressions of the imperial theme: *Isabela* a "sentimental" expression, *St. Agnes' Eve* a "romantic", *The Eve of St. Mark* a "cheated", and *Lamia* a "cynical". . . . There is no doubt of Keats's growing interest in the darker aspects of the love relationship. *Lamia* is a presentation of love as obsession and as degradation. . . . Keats has already begun to explore it . . . in *La Belle Dame Sans Merci*. . . . We can have no doubt that it was the morbidity and ambiguity of his passion for Fanny Brawne – a passion he fought against the more it "entrammelled" him – which led him into this area of thought, the area of the sedgeless lake and the cold hill-side.[2]

I have difficulty in following the logic of this argument. I do not understand how a combination of economic, financial, and other essentially social pressures which frustrate the consummation of sexual passion will necessarily lead to a denunciation of the passion itself. Had Keats married Fanny Brawne and then discovered that the pleasures of the marriage bed were not quite all that he had imagined in his early poetry, then such a transformation might make more sense. But from what we know of the circumstances surrounding the frustrated young Keats – the fact that he had no money, that Fanny was a respectable if somewhat flirtatious female with no intense feelings toward her passionate young admirer and no intentions of embarking upon a romantic interlude with

---

[1] Bernard Blackstone, *The Consecrated Urn* (London, Longman's, Green, 1959), p. 281.
[2] *Ibid.*, pp. 298-299.

him, the fact that family, economic, and social pressure seemed to
combine in a vast conspiracy against the ultimate realization of his
desires – all of these factors might well join to leave him in a
frustrated, agonized condition with little hope of escape. But such
conditions do not seem likely to lead to insight. They might, however, lead to a bitter and intense hatred of the forces that seemed
in league against him.

As we read these two poems then, *La Belle Dame* and *Lamia*,
we should look for some fairly definite signs that Keats meant us
to see the symbols of Eros as destructive and evil; and in my
reading of the poems, I find little evidence that the symbols have
been so re-evaluated. The communicant at love's shrine is destroyed in both poems, certainly, but the destroyer is not the love
goddess.

The mysterious lady from the "elfin grot" in *La Belle Dame* is
not defined in the imagery of the poem itself as evil or destructive.
Although she is a mythic figure with literary ancestors stretching
back at least as far as Spenser's Acrasia, it does not necessarily
follow that Keats is using the mythic figure in his poem in the
traditional manner. Keats may be doing something with myth
other than merely recasting it into a different form. As Earl
Wasserman has rightly observed, the myth is not "merely an
esthetic design that he felt he could bring closer to his idea of
literary perfection".[3] It is far more than this. For Keats this figure
might have offered a meaningful pattern into which he could
project his own attitudes toward the obviously erotic forces for
which she is a symbol.

There seems little if any evidence in the language of the poem to
suggest that the lady is simply destructive. The idea that she is a
vampire, sucking the life blood from the knight-at-arms, is
absurd.[4] Nothing happens to the knight while he is with the lady.
Nor does the argument of Francis Utley, that the actions of La
Belle Dame are "infernal strategies", motivated by a conscious

---

[3]   Earl Wasserman, *The Finer Tone* (Baltimore, Johns Hopkins Press,
1953), p. 59.
[4]   Edwin R. Clapp, "La Belle Dame as Vampire", *PQ*, XXVII (1948),
pp. 89-92.

and malevolent attempt to do evil, seem supported by the poem.[5]

E. C. Pettet, realizing that this kind of interpretation is an inadequate over-simplification, nonetheless supports it finally. He finds it difficult, as I do, to see how the Keats who described the transforming power of sensual love in *Endymion* and *Eve of St. Agnes* "could so completely reverse himself here and write a poem denouncing sensuous love as baneful and sinister".[6] But seeing the poem as the poetic crystallization of Keats' ambiguous, half-crazed feelings toward Fanny, Pettet, like the others, decides that "one thing at least is clear enough in the poem: that is the re-emergence from *La Belle Dame Sans Merci* of the theme of love's fatality".[7] Like most commentators on the poem, he finally judges the enchantress herself as sinister, failing to see that the theme of love's fatality is not necessarily present in the language of the poem.

For, as Earl Wasserman has so perceptively shown in his reading of the ballad, the female enchantress in this poem is not *simply* the baleful, destructive figure of the traditional poems of enchantment. He rightly observes that "there is nothing in Keats' ballad even suggesting the frequent interpretation that the fairy's child is responsible for the knight's expulsion from the elfin grot; only his inherent attribute of being mortal causes his magic withdrawal".[8] The knight, being mortal, aspired to the condition of immortality; but having reached this immortal world, "the elfin grot", he must leave again:

All mortals who engage in "Imagination's struggles" are knights-at-arms. But man cannot gain his quest in this world. No knights-at-arms can remain in the elfin grot because, since he is mortal, he cannot wholly yield himself up to this extra-human realm and gain visionary insight into its nature. He will be impelled to make the visionary physical or will long for "his friend so long forgot". It is man's bond with mankind that prevents him from lingering beyond the bourne of care.[9]

---

[5] Francis L. Utley, "La Belle Dame and the Inferno of Lucretius", *ELH*, XXV (1958), p. 118.
[6] E. C. Pettet, *On the Poetry of Keats*, p. 216.
[7] *Ibid.*, p. 229.
[8] Wasserman, p. 74.
[9] *Ibid.*, p. 75.

The only sense in which the fairy's child is without *merci* is that she represents the unattainable: the immortal world which all men of imagination yearn for but which can only be reached after death. There is nothing evil in the figure herself, according to Wasserman.

Such an evaluation of the lady's character is obvious in any detailed examination of the poem itself. The first three stanzas present the knight as a figure of desolation: he is alone and "palely loitering" in a landscape withered and dead. This desolation of the landscape is heightened magnificently by the single line at the end of the first stanza: "And no birds sing". The second stanza reinforces the image of the knight's condition in the first two lines: again, he is "haggard and so woe-begone". A contrast is implied between this autumnal state of the knight, dying like the flowers at the end of summer (the fading rose that "fast withereth"), and the fullness of autumn in the natural world. In contrast to the knight, the natural world is full of abundance: "the squirrel's granary is full/ And the harvest's done". The knight is on the verge of death: his condition approximates the superficial appearance of nature with its withered sedge and birdless landscape; but at the same time a contrast is established between the world of the knight, man's world which is fading at autumn, and the world of nature which overflows with abundance at autumn.

In the fourth stanza, the knight replies to the questioner, explaining how he came to such a sorry state:

> I met a lady in the meads,
> Full beautiful – a faery's child,
> Her hair was long, her foot was light,
> And her eyes were wild.

The poem gives us no further details of the lady's appearance.

The knight still refers to her as a "lady", with all the connotations and suggestions of gentility and chivalry the word implies. He is recounting the story of his encounter and surely by this time should have some indications of her supposedly evil nature, if she is to be seen as evil.

The encounter took place in the "meads" or meadows, an open space far removed from the forests and jungles traditionally haunt-

ed by such evil creatures. In the manuscript of the poem, Keats
had originally written "wilds" as the place of the meeting but lined
it out in favor of the more pleasant "meads", suggesting a deliberate attempt to soften the circumstances surrounding the meeting.
Nor does the term "faery's child" imply anything necessarily evil:
certainly all supernatural creatures, especially supernatural creatures in Keats' verse, are not to be automatically considered as
evil or sinister.

In short, no indisputably evil characteristics seem to be inherent
in La Belle Dame's physical appearance. She is a beautiful lady
from fairy land, encountered in the lush abundant meadows. The
lady has long hair, is light of carriage, "and her eyes were wild".
Now, though the wildness of her eyes may indicate a certain
savagery or animality, they need not, as Utley suggests, imply
conscious malevolence.[10] *Wild* can also mean untamed or un-
civilized, an indication that she is not a part of the "tame" world
of civilization from which the knight has come. It might even
suggest that the knight is about to undergo some experience not a
part of his role as "knight-at-arms", attached to the public and
civilized society of courts, kings, and feudal loyalties.

It is important to remember in this context that later the knight
shuts her "wild, wild eyes/ With kisses four". The love-making in
the elfin grot leads to some modification of the wildness: the
closing of her eyes suggests such a softening. The lady becomes
tamer, less a creature of the wilds, when possessed by man.

The following stanzas describe the acts of love, tracing the
progress of the knight's enchantment. As Wasserman has pointed
out, there is a gradual shrinking during this enchantment of the
"I" and a corresponding growth in power of the "She".[11] His
suggestion that this progression represents a movement toward the
heights of Keats' pleasure thermometer is interesting, but more to
the point here is the indication that the knight, gradually, through
his own choice, is moving away from the world dominated by the
egocentric "I" to a world in which the "I" becomes submerged in

[10]   Utley, p. 119.
[11]   Wasserman, pp. 78-79.

the identity of the loved one. Stanzas four, five, and six describe actions of the knight: "I met a lady on the meads . . .", "I made a garland for her head . . .", and "I set her on my pacing steed". But the next three stanzas show the lady as the active force. In response to the knight's actions, "She found me . . . roots of relish sweet . . .", "She took me . . . to her elfin grot . . .", and ". . . there she lulled me . . . to sleep". It is not until stanza nine, after the knight has been lulled asleep, that the egocentric "I" returns to the poem. And the "I" dreams the terrible dream:

> And there I dreamed – Ah! woe betide!
> The latest dream I ever dream'd
> On the cold hill side.

This shrinkage and re-emergence of the "I" emphasizes that the knight and his actions are the most significant actions in the poem. What the knight does, what he sees, and what he makes of the encounter are more important than the activities of the enchantress. The episode is initiated by the knight.

Not until the knight woos her does she act. She appears before him, he courts her, then she responds to him. She is essentially passive, her only active gestures are a "look" and a "sweet moan".

This pattern is repeated in the next stanza: again the knight initiates the action.

> I set her on my pacing steed[12]
> And nothing else saw all day long.

As La Belle Dame gradually becomes the active agent in the poem, her actions still carry no connotations of sinister or evil motives. She gathers strange and delicious food for the knight:

> She found me roots of relish sweet
> And honey wild, and manna dew.

Utley finds in this scene the folk-tale motif of mortal destruction as the result of eating food in the other world. The manna, food dropped from heaven, is not, according to Utley, true manna, but

[12] Cf. "Thomas the Rhymer", often cited as one of the primary sources for *La Belle Dame Sans Merci*, in which the Queen of Elfland takes the hero upon *her* "milk-white steed".

"false manna . . . really not from heaven but created for the occasion by one of hell's creatures for the Knight's destruction".[13] But surely this "manna dew" is true food from heaven, indicating that the knight has joined the select circle of the blessed. In the *Eve of St. Agnes*, after all, one of the foods Porphyro prepares for Madeline in the banquet scene in the bed chamber is manna. There certainly is no causal relationship indicated in the poem between the manna dew and the destruction of the knight.

After the lady takes the knight to the "elfin grot", she gives every indication that she feels real sorrow for the knight's predicament, that she may even be aware that their remaining together is a tragic impossibility, that she is full of concern about the fate she perhaps knows is about to overtake the knight. The lady's weeping and sighing has nothing of the counterfeit about it: "And there she wep't and sigh'd full sore." In fact, if she is a malevolent creature from hell, why should she carry on in this manner? She has already accomplished the knight's destruction by enticing him to the elfin grot.

Nothing evil happens to the knight while he is in the elfin grot. Not until he is lulled asleep and dreams does evil overtake him. The causal element in the knight's predicament at the beginning of the poem seems to be related far more closely to the dream than to the enchantment. As we shall see, the dream produces the desolation: by dreaming, he loses lady, elfin grot, and life.

Now this dream, the "latest dream" of the knight, is admittedly puzzling. The knight has been lulled to sleep in the elfin grot, but the dream transports him to the cold hill side. He falls asleep in Elfland, traditionally associated with the world of imaginative dream fantasy, but is transformed back to what seems to be the real world by the dream. This action should be contrasted with the dreaming of Endymion, in which the dream transports him to the equivalent in that poem of the elfin grot, the immortal world of the goddess. The cold hill side is the equivalent of the bleak world in which Endymion discovers himself upon being awakened from the dream. And, of course, in *Eve of St. Agnes*, Madeline dreams and the dream becomes the reality; Porphyro melts into her dream.

In *La Belle Dame*, however, the knight's account of his experience in the elfin grot does not seem to be a dream; it may have occurred in an imaginative world, but this is not the same as a dream world. The dream here is of pale kings and warriors warning him of his danger, and it is a nightmare. Moreover, through dreaming, he has been ejected from the elfin grot. This is a dramatic shift in the symbolic pattern associated with dreaming, and has never been pointed out in connection with this poem. Such a shift suggests an entirely new concept of reality for Keats, different from the earlier poems: a concept which sees the imaginative world of the elfin grot as real and the supposedly real world as the illusion. "What the imagination seizes upon as Beauty must be Truth whether it existed before or not", Keats has written in a letter to Baily; and the *Ode on a Grecian Urn* ends with the same affirmation: "Beauty is Truth, Truth Beauty".

This new dream-world, better named the "nightmare-world", is a powerful one, capable of destroying the imaginative reality of the elfin grot. And this capacity to destroy is emphasized as the poem continues.

> I saw pale kings and princes too,
> Pale warriors, death-pale were they all;
> They cried – "La Belle Dame Sans Merci
> Hath thee in thrall."
>
> I saw their starved lips in the gloam,
> With horrid warning gaped wide
> And I awoke and found me here
> On the cold hill's side.

Pettet describes these lines as a "terrifying dream revelation, of love as a cruel destroyer ... the knight knows himself to be a victim: he is alone and dying in a world of death and winter desolation".[14] I am not at all sure, however, that what these lines show is "love as a cruel destroyer". Love is not doing the destroying here; love is still back in the elfin grot. The destroyers are in fact the pale kings and princes.

[14] Pettet, pp. 214-215.

They may be previous victims of the lady who have undergone a similar experience, and they may even be trying to save the knight through their "horrid warning". But surely "horrid warning" must be read on at least two levels. First of all it is a warning, even a prediction of what is about to happen. In this sense it is a warning of horrid things about to happen as a result of the knight's enchantment. But, on another level, it is horrid because it is capable of destroying the imaginative world of the elfin grot, and in fact it is the warning that does destroy it.

The central figures in this dream are the kings and princes, representatives of the world which passes for reality, the nightmare-world. They are the public figures of this world, the leaders of the feudal society. Like Madeline's family in *Eve of St. Agnes*, like the great historical personages Endymion is called upon to emulate by the practical Peona, like the relentlessly rational Appollonius who destroys the beautiful Lamia, they are love's enemies. The knight, too, is a member of this world, a "knight-at-arms", who owes his feudal loyalties to this world. And it is from this nightmare world that the beautiful enchantress has tried to rescue him.

From the point of view of the kings and princes, La Belle Dame and her elfin grot are evil, the enchantment of the knight-at-arms is destructive, and their duty is to warn him, to release him from the enchantment even if it kills him. They are not simply the victims of La Belle Dame; they are her enemies. It is not completely accidental that these pale warriors give the enchantress her name. To them she is *La Belle Dame Sans Merci*, an evil, destructive, merciless witch who has trapped the unwary knight and subverted him from his true loyalties. The horrible irony of their warning is that their intrusion destroys the knight as well as the lady: they are the responsible agents for the knight's subsequent desolation and withered state.

The last stanza of the poem makes the point starkly clear:

> And *this* is why I sojourn here,
> Alone and palely loitering,
> Though the sedge has wither'd from the lake
> And no birds sing.

The pronoun "this" refers to the "horrid warning" and the dream which has destroyed the elfin grot: it does not refer to his total experience with La Belle Dame. He is alone and palely loitering because he has been called back to rejoin the "pale" world of the pale warriors. Having tasted of Paradise or its equivalent, he is incapacitated for his former activities as a knight-at-arms. The nightmare world is even more desolate than before, for he has learned that life can be more than a nightmare.

Keats' attitude toward the erotic has not changed in *La Belle Dame Sans Merci*. La Belle Dame is still the same passionate, sensual goddess of the early poems, though her erotic qualities are somewhat played down here. Her ancestry may at first make her somewhat suspect, but there is far more than a hint here that Keats is deliberately trying to *reverse* the traditional evaluation of such an enchantress. Perhaps realizing that the old versions of the myth, in accordance with a rather fixed and static moral vision, tended to denigrate the forces of eros, Keats deliberately chose a figure traditionally associated with evil. But also realizing the ineffectiveness of this static moral vision as a means of describing or effectively coping with erotic feeling, he is trying to demonstrate here that it is not the dedication to Eros that destroys. The destructive element is the role we play as knights-at-arms. The world, the nightmare-world of the pale kings and warriors, is too much with us. And this world successfully prevents us from realizing the possibilities of love's fulfillment in the elfin grot.

The new awareness Keats demonstrates in *La Belle Dame* is that the enemies of love are stronger than he had previously thought. Unlike the drunken revelers in Madeline's castle, they are now awake; and they shout their horrid warnings to the errant knight whether he wishes to listen or not. But the warning does not save him – it only destroys.

The new theme that emerges here is the theme of love's defeat, not of love's fatality. Dedication to love no longer serves as a means to defeat the forces opposed to it. But this does not indicate a shift away from the previous concept of love as a positive and eternal value in human affairs. Love is less powerful, its foes more numerous and stronger; and the ultimate triumph of love is no longer certain. This theme is taken up again and given extended treatment in the last of Keats' great love poems, *Lamia*.

This long narrative poem of seduction and enchantment has been used as key illustration by those critics who wish to demonstrate Keats' growth from the mere singer of love's pleasure to the "mature" commentator upon love's snares. The poem seems to lend itself to such a reading for several reasons; the symbolic figure of reason, old Apollonius, kills the seductress; the symbol of sensual and erotic love is a serpent, although a beautiful serpent; and, of course, the poem ends tragically with the death of the protagonist. An apparent cause and effect relationship seems to exist between seduction and destruction.

It would be tedious and irrelevant to review in detail the catalogue of critics whose comments on the poem focus on pointing out the evil of Lamia, the innocence and naivete of Lycius, and the firm and resolute nature of Apollonius. Clarence D. Thorpe's analysis is typical.

According to Thorpe, the poem represents the culmination of Keats' intellectual development, the high point of the young poet's awareness. Although Apollonius, the old philosopher, is responsible for the death of the sensual Lamia, he cannot represent reason as such, argues Thorpe, because Keats had too high a regard for reason to treat it so unsympathetically. Therefore, Thorpe allegorizes the poem: it is an allegory of the poet's life; the beautiful pleasure palace Lamia constructs in Corinth is the palace of the unreflective dreams of youth. Lamia is only "apparently beautiful", a serpent in disguise, representing "mere sensuous passion, feeling without knowledge, empty dreams". Apollonius, "cold philosophy", the old dream destroyer, is Keats' self-criticism, his awakened intellect; through his intervention, "the false Duessa" fades away and the palace falls. "The youngster who loves so unwisely also dies – though in its place is born a stronger, firmer soul." [15] This is ingenious but ignores the fact that in the poem no such stronger, firmer soul is left. The destruction of Lamia by Apollonius causes the death of Lycius. If the influence

[15]   Clarence D. Thorpe, *The Mind of John Keats*, p. 102.

of Lamia over Lycius is evil, to be removed like a cancerous growth, we ought to hope for a healthier patient after surgery. But an operation in which the patient dies can hardly be called a success; and Apollonius' surgical technique seems a little clumsy. Furthermore, Thorpe's reading of the poem completely ignores the fact that Keats seems to go out of his way to eliminate the evil connotations traditionally surrounding the figure of the serpent.

Among other critics whose conclusions about the nature of the serpent woman are essentially the same as Thorpe's, are H. W. Garrod, who insists that she is evil because she is a snake and snakes are evil; [16] R. D. Havens, who demands that Apollonius be seen as the deliverer from evil and Lamia be seen as "a snake, a deceiver, with powers of dubious origin"; [17] and Newell Ford, who claims that in Lamia, Keats is demonstrating that sensual beauty "however entrancing and highly to be treasured, is only 'aery nothing' ".[18]

Actually, one of the more traditional commentators on the poem, Sidney Colvin, comes the closest to reading the poem straight. Colvin, who could allegorize the life out of *Endymion* and read Platonic intentions into *The Eve of St. Agnes*, is frankly puzzled over the meaning of Lamia. He sees what Keats is getting at but cannot face the awful truth:

> ... the one fundamental flaw in *Lamia* concerns its moral ... what I mean is the bewilderment in which it leaves us as to the effect intended to be made on our imaginative sympathies. Lamia is a serpent woman, baleful and a witch, whose love for Lycius fills him with momentary happiness but must, we are made aware, be fatal to him. Apollonius is a philosopher who sees through her and by one steadfast look withers up her magic semblance and destroys her, but in doing so fails to save his pupil, who dies the moment his illusion vanishes.. Are these things a bitter parable of universal application, meaning that all love-joys are but deception and at the touch of wisdom and experience they melt away? Why are we asked to take sides with the enchantress, ignoring everything about her except her charm, and

---

[16]   H. W. Garrod, *Keats* (Oxford, Clarendon Press, 1926), p. 62.

[17]   R. D. Havens, "Of Beauty and Reality in Keats", *ELH*, XVII (1950), p. 209.

[18]   Newell F. Ford, *The Prefigurative Imagination of John Keats*, p. 144.

against the sage? ... Is there not in all this a slackening of imaginative and intellectual grasp? ... It is a cheap and unilluminating repetition of a rather superficial idea ... not fit to stand in serious poetry.[19]

This is strong but honest language. Colvin, a moralist dedicated to the proposition that a life of the mind is the highest state that a man might aspire to, realizes what Keats is doing. Although the statement shows Colvin's rationalistic bias, he makes no attempt to force Keats into this company.

It is interesting, in fact, to analyze the language of Colvin's remarks, contrasting them with Keats' actual practice in the poem. Colvin calls Lamia a baleful witch, but "baleful" and "witch" are Colvin's terms, not Keats'. At no time during the poem is she described as a witch, nor are her actions anything that might be identified as "baleful". The "steadfast look" which Colvin says Apollonius directs toward Lamia is apparently what the language of the poem calls "the sophist's eye", an eye that is earlier "without a twinkle or stir" fixed upon the beauty of the bride, "browbeating her fair form and troubling her sweet pride". "Steadfast" is hardly the correct word to define the "keen, cruel, perceant, stinging" eye that destroys both Lamia and Lycius, the eye that represents the "mere touch of cold philosophy". I am not quite sure what this proves other than that Colvin's Apollonius is different from Keats'. They may both be symbolic figures of philosophical and rationalistic thought, but Colvin likes what the symbol stands for far more than Keats seems to.

Actually, as I hope to demonstrate in my analysis, the figure of Lamia is treated sympathetically throughout the poem. She, like Cynthia, Madeline, and La Belle Dame, quite obviously symbolizes the erotic, the figure worshipped by the male protagonists of the preceding poems. And, like La Belle Dame, she is involved in a series of events which lead to the destruction of the worshipper. But the force responsible for the destruction is external to the relationship and the worship. Just as the external forces have destroyed the "elfin grot", they now destroy the pleasure palace.

Previous studies of the poem have tended to concentrate almost

[19] Sidney Colvin, *John Keats*, pp. 407-408.

exclusively upon the relationship of Lycius and Lamia and its tragic conclusion. With the exception of Earl Wasserman, no one has paid much attention to the first 145 lines of the poem in which Lamia in serpent form aids Hermes in his search for an evasive nymph. Wasserman tries to integrate this brief interlude, which also serves as an introduction, with the rest of the poem. He feels that the love of Hermes for the nymph provides a kind of contrast for the love of Lamia and Lycius. Both Hermes and the nymph are gods, immortals, who can enjoy an immortality of passion because of their godlike state. Theirs is the dream world of ideal beauty, a heaven of perfect attainment where love is forever warm.

But Lycius, being mortal, cannot attain such perfection; he may catch a fleeting glimpse of the ideal in dreams and visions, but he must return to earth. Hermes and the nymph exist in a world where the vision of the ideal is real: a world where beauty is truth. Wasserman calls this introductory episode "a hypothesis of perfection, an ideal against which he [Keats] may examine and understand the life of mortal man . . . It is Keats' intention . . . to sharpen the outlines of Lycius' tragedy by painting it against a background of precisely the same events experienced under immortal, and therefore perfect, conditions." [20]

To some extent the Hermes episode can be seen as this: there is certainly an implied, even a direct contrast, between the tragedy of Lycius and the immortal lovers who fly away into the "green-recessed woods" to enjoy in undisturbed fidelity the fruits of their passion. The immortals are to be eternally happy, "nor grew they pale, as mortal lovers do", while the love of Lycius and Lamia is doomed to destruction. But I wonder if this implied contrast between the two kinds of love, mortal and immortal, is the main point of this passage. It seems to me to neglect the presence of Lamia who, in her role as serpent, makes the union of Hermes and nymph possible. The contrast between the two sets of lovers is certainly there, but is this contrast to be read in quite the same way Wasserman reads it? After all, it is Lamia's presence in both narratives that ties them together; and it is Lamia's power in the Hermes-nymph relationship that makes their immortality of passion possible. Furthermore, the destruction of her power through the old philosopher causes the tragedy.

Wasserman admits that he does not understand the full significance of Lamia in this section:

> I am forced to confess that I cannot fathom the full significance of Lamia's origin or of her terribly splendid transformation into a beautiful woman. Nor do I understand why it is she who governs the visibility of the nymph, and yet requires the aid of Hermes to become metamorphosed into a woman.[21]

But if we can see Lamia's significance, perhaps we will realize that it is precisely her power over the nymph and Hermes, as well as over Lycius, that provides the focal point of the action.

The poem opens by making a contrast: a contrast between two different kinds of imaginative and mythic worlds. The action of this poem takes place long ago in some dim past:

> . . . before the faery broods
> Drove Nymph and Satyr from the prosperous woods;
> Before King Oberon's bright diadem
> Sceptre, and mantle, clasp'd with dewy gem,
> Frighted away the Dryads and the Fauns. (I, 1-5)

Now I'm not completely certain what distinction Keats intends to make here between these two kinds of imaginary creatures; but the sexual, somewhat barbarous nature of Nymphs, Fauns, Satyrs, and Dryads is obvious. This sexuality is emphasized in the description of the nymph who had cast her love's spell over all the creatures of the woods: creatures whose subsequent hot pursuit had necessitated Lamia's robing the nymph in a cloak of invisibility.

Not even the Olympian gods are exempt from the nymph's charms and enchantment: the description of the "ever-smitten Hermes" burning with celestial heat in his passionate search for the nymph is one of the most memorable in the poem:

---

[21] *Ibid.*, p. 165.

> ... a celestial heat
> Burnt from his winged heels to either ear
> That from a whiteness, as the lily clear,
> Blush'd into roses 'mid his golden hair,
> Fallen in jealous curls about his shoulders bare.
> From vale to vale, from wood to wood, he flew
> Breathing upon the flowers his passion new
> And wound with many a river to its head
> To find where this sweet nymph prepar'd her secret bed.
>
> (I, 22-30)

If the Nymphs and Satyrs are to be taken as symbols of passionate, intense, burning, and in some cases "unlovely" love, then the "faery brood" of the first line must refer to a newer, less passionate realm of the imagination. King Oberon with his *"bright diadem,* sceptre and mantle" which had frightened away these rude creatures, is perhaps symbolic of some kind of authority and order. The action of the poem, of the first section at least, takes place in a time and place before the existence of such authority.

Sensual passion seems to dominate this anarchic world. The nymph is forced to hide in order to escape the passionate embraces of this motley crew; and Lamia's power helps her to escape. As Lamia reveals to Hermes later in the narrative,

> ... by my power is her beauty veil'd
> To keep it unaffronted, unassail'd
> By the love-glances of unlovely eyes,
> Of Satyrs, Fauns, and blear'd Silenus' sighs.
> Pale grew her immortality, for woe
> Of all these lovers, and she grieved so
> I took compassion on her, bade her steep
> Her hair in weird syrops, that would keep
> Her loveliness invisible, yet free
> To wander as she loves, in liberty. (I, 100-109)

However, in return for Hermes' promise to restore her woman's shape, Lamia is perfectly willing to turn the nymph over to him; nor is his "burning" for the nymph any less passionate than the burnings of the Satyrs and Fauns before him. No ideal of chastity or self-denial operates in this case: the nymph had been saved *for* Hermes, not *from* ravishment or sexual passion:

> ... upon the nymph his eyes he bent
> Full of adoring tears and blandishment,
> And towards her stept: she, like a moon in wane,
> Faded before him, cower'd, nor could restrain
> Her fearful sobs, self-folding like a flower
> That faints into itself at evening hour:
> But the God fostering her chilled hand,
> She felt the warmth, her eyelids open'd bland,
> And, like new flowers at morning song of bees,
> Bloom'd and gave up her honey to the lees. (I, 134-143)

Now just what is this power of Lamia's? It is a strange power, for the other gods do not possess it: Hermes was doomed to burn in vain until Lamia releases the nymph. It dominates the Satyr-world in which both she and nymph reside; it can be used to protect from passion as well as open the doors to passion; and it is obviously a somewhat limited power. For although she can make the love between Hermes and nymph possible, she cannot transform herself into a different shape, nor later in the poem can she protect herself from the withering eye of Apollonius. However, she can erect a beautiful palace of love in the midst of nowhere and create a vision of love which becomes necessary for the continued existence of Lycius. Her power, apparently confined to the realm of love and lovers, dreams and visions, is powerless to change itself or reality.

The early lines of the poem, before and during her transformation from snake to woman, give us considerable clues to the significance of this power and the significance of Lamia in the poem. Our first contact with her comes when Hermes, resting from his frenzied search, hears her voice:

> There as he stood, he heard a mournful voice,
> Such as once heard, in gentle heart, destroys
> All pain but pity: thus the lone voice spake:
> "When from this wreathed tomb shall I awake!
> When move in a sweet body fit for life,
> And love, and pleasure, and the ruddy strife
> Of hearts and lips! Ah miserable me!" (I, 35-41)

Now I think we must look at these lines closely, trying to determine as nearly as possible the exact effect Keats meant to create by introducing this title character in such a fashion. First of all, the quality of the voice: it is "mournful", a "lone voice", a voice which destroys "*in gentle heart* . . . all pain but pity". We do not know at this point that the speaker is a serpent: all we know is that a voice is speaking, a sorrowful voice which does not ask for pity, but arouses pity. The voice is, furthermore, beautiful, later described as one that "came, as through bubbling honey, for Love's sake".

As for Lamia's lines, upon close analysis they reveal some interesting aspects of her real nature. She refers to her body, that which we subsequently learn is the body of a snake, as a "wreathed tomb". She enquires, piteously, when she will "awake" from this tomb. She wishes to be removed into a "sweet body fit for life and love and pleasure, and the ruddy strife of hearts and lips". We see her then as a captive, a spirit entombed in a body she wishes to change. The implication is strong that the serpent body is something extraneous to the voice speaking: the real self is the voice – the serpent body holds this self captive. This point is emphasized later when the serpent body is described in all of its beautiful, glowing, gem-like color:

> She *seemed*, at once, some penanced lady elf,
> Some demon's mistress, or the demon's self. (I, 56-57)

The important word here is, of course, *seemed* (which I have italicized): the serpent's form causes her to *seem* evil; it does not make her a demon or a demon's mistress.

The description continues, drawing contrast between the body, even the head, and the mouth and eyes:

> Her head was serpent, but ah, bitter-sweet!
> She had a woman's mouth with all its pearls complete:
> And for her eyes: what could such eyes do there
> But weep, and weep, that they were born so fair? (I, 59-62)

Finally, when she has extracted from Hermes the oath to grant her boon, we learn that the serpent's body is indeed not her natural shape. For as she informs Hermes:

> I was a woman, let me have once more
> A woman's shape, and charming as before.

I love a youth of Corinth – O the bliss!
Give me my woman's form, and place me where he is.
(I, 117-120)

Apparently, then, Lamia is not really a serpent. By those who
read the poem simply, this central fact seems to have been ignored.
She has obviously been changed into a serpent by some process,
not clear in the poem; but she is not now nor has she ever been a
serpent, *qua* serpent. The serpent form she has been forced to
take has indeed been a "wreathed tomb"; the body which she
eventually puts on and with which she wins the love of Lycius is
presumably her real form. She is not a serpent in female form, but
in the early part of the poem she is a woman, forced through some
spell, it would seem, to wear the form of a serpent. She is obviously not an ordinary woman, that much is clear: she possesses supernatural attributes along with her great beauty. But she is primarily
woman – not primarily serpent.

Thus the Lamia of whom Lycius subsequently becomes en-
amored is not a disguised serpent – the woman's form is her true
form. The serpent form is the form symbolic of death and the
tomb – the true form, the form of woman, is equated with life, "a
sweet body fit for life,/ And love, and pleasure, and the ruddy
strife/ Of hearts and lips".

Apollonius, when he calls her a serpent, shows the limitations
of reason. He sees only the false form, that which Lamia has been
permitted to throw off in payment for aiding Hermes in love's
cause. Actually, the old philosopher is undoing the work of the
gods, destroying that which is love's reward. He means well, just
as the knights and warriors of *La Belle Dame* believe they are
saving the knight from destruction, or Peona believes she is giving
the love-smitten Endymion good advice. But the results of these
good intentions are catastrophic. Apollonius does not reveal to
Lycius the true nature of Lamia; he only destroys her. He does
not open his student's eyes; he only closes them, finally and
permanently.

If, then, Lamia is not a witch, a serpent in woman's form, what
is she? And what is the mysterious power she exerts? We have
seen her somewhat mystically identified with love; she can protect

the innocent from "unlovely" love and yet has the power to grant the attainment of love – she is the instrument which allows Hermes and the nymph to enjoy the passionate consummation of their love without fading or growing pale as is the case with mortal lovers. In the savage world of nymphs and satyrs, she must wear the body of a snake, but when the "barbarous rout" of primitive passion has been displaced by the gentle, passionate, but no less sensual love of Hermes for the nymph, Lamia is transformed. She is, in fact, freed from her "wreathed tomb" almost simultaneously with the possession of the nymph by Hermes. The two acts seem to be connected. Lamia's serpent form, in strange contrast to the beautiful mouth, eyes, and voice, is associated only with a primitive satyr world in which love and carnal passion are identical. In this world the nature of Lamia is ambiguous: the beauty of the serpent is latent in this primitive world; but not until love becomes divine, until Hermes and the nymph are united, are the brutish aspects of carnal love transformed into the gentle sensuality of the two immortal lovers.

Lamia's change in form is symbolic of this transformation of love. What may have been ugly and bestial is now beautiful and fully human. The love of Hermes for the nymph, although divine, can be transposed to earth. Just as the satyr world disappears with the advent of Hermes, the snake's body falls away and the true form emerges. Lamia is not only a love-goddess, she is the very spirit of human love emerging from the world of primitive passion, changing the satyr world through her influence and, now with the help of the gods, bringing this new concept of love to man.

The transformation from serpent to woman is a terrible, painful process; all of evolution accomplished in a few moments:

> Her mouth foam'd and the grass, therewith besprent
> Wither'd at dew so sweet and virulent;
> Her eyes in torture fix'd, and anguish drear,
> Hot, glaz'd, and wide, with lid-lashes all sear,
> Flash'd phosphor and sharp sparks, without one
>   cooling tear.]
> The colours all inflam'd throughout her train,
> She writh'd about, convuls'd with scarlet pain:
> A deep volcanian yellow took the place

> Of all her milder-mooned body's grace;
> And as the lava ravishes the mead,
> Spoilt all her silver mail, and golden brede,
> Made gloom of all her frecklings, streaks and bars,
> Eclips'd her crescents, and lick'd up her stars:
> So that, in moments few, she was undrest
> Of all her sapphires, greens, and amethyst,
> And rubious-argent: of all these bereft,
> Nothing but pain and ugliness were left.
> Still shone her crown; that vanish'd, also she
> Melted and disappear'd as suddenly; (I, 148-166)

The beautiful, brilliant serpent body is destroyed; and the moment before the transformation is complete, before Lamia vanishes from the immortal world, nothing is left but "pain and ugliness". If these lines suggest that under the barbaric splendor of the serpent something ugly exists, it must also be remembered that the ugliness exists just before the transformation is complete. And as the halo-like crown disappears, the pain and ugliness presumably disappear along with the serpent form:

> . . . that vanished, also, she
> Melted and disappeared as suddenly. (I, 164-165)

As her voice cries out for "Lycius, gentle Lycius", Lamia disappears from the immortal world and moves into the sphere of man to offer him the opportunity of redemption through love.

This is the Lamia who greets Lycius as he returns to Corinth fresh from sacrificing to Jove:

> . . . a maid
> More beautiful than ever twisted braid,
> Or sighed, or blushed, or on the spring-flowered lea
> Spread a green kirtle to the minstrelsy:
> A virgin purest lipp'd, *yet in the lore*
> *Of love deep learned to the red heart's core:*
> Not one hour old, yet of sciential brain
> To unperplex bliss from its neighbor pain. (I, 184-192)

Wasserman claims that this new Lamia is contaminated by her previous form, that she is, as he puts it,

a kind of earthly version of Cynthia . . . as Cynthia-like as Cynthia can be in the mortal world, for here beauty and ugliness, pleasure and pain, are inseparable. And the Lamia with whom the poem begins is that dualism, a beauty of the world, a Cynthia-serpent.[22]

But Wasserman fails to see either the symbolism of the serpent form, as a tomb of the spirit, or the significance of the new Lamia, released from the "wreathed tomb". The new Lamia is the spirit of essence entombed in the satyr world, but now released. This spirit, manifest before only in the beautiful voice, has never been defined as evil.

Nothing in the description of Lamia after her transformation indicates that her beauty is treacherous or that her love is false. When she encounters Lycius and enchants him with her beauty, had Keats meant to indicate that the temptress was tainted by evil or that the consequences of giving in to the enchantress were bad, he could have done so. But we find no such indication. As Lycius passes, having just completed his sacrifices to Jove, he is wrapped in thought, lost in "the calm'd twilight of Platonic shades" – certainly a somewhat ironic reference to the influence of Apollonius. Lamia calls to him, breaking his Platonic reverie:

> Ah Lycius bright
> And will you leave me on the hills alone?
> Lycius look back! and be some pity shown.

Now if the encounter with Lamia were to be seen as essentially evil, her appearance to a youth purified from sacrifices to the gods must be seen as a consummate piece of irony. She appears, in fact, immediately after his sacrifice to Jove, which has been acknowledged: "Jove heard his vows and better'd his desire." This is strikingly similar to Geraldine's appearance following Christabel's prayers for her lover. Is her appearance at this point an indication that in response to his sacrifice and prayer he is rewarded by a destructive encounter with an evil force? Or is it more likely that Lamia, a goddess-like creature from the immortal world, comes to Lycius as an answer to his prayer? She is offering to Lycius the same opportunity for love's fulfillment that she had previously offered to Hermes. And, as the poem develops, it be-

---

[22]   *Ibid.*, p. 166.

comes apparent that Lycius muffs his chance. He is given the opportunity but, unlike Endymion, he falls far short of the complete devotion to the goddess who could guarantee his erotic salvation. And, more importantly, the powers of the world in this poem are immeasurably more effective in combatting the erotic spirit.

The entire temptation scene supports the idea that Lamia is offering to Lycius something valuable, that she represents something new and beautiful, something originating in sensual love but differing from the usual sensual activity in exactly the same way that Hermes' love for the nymph differs from the Satyrs'. Like Hermes, Lycius *hears* the goddess first. She calls to him; and Lycius, before he ever sees her, is enamoured by the sound of her voice. He looks back toward the voice:

> . . . not in cold wonder dearingly,
> But Orpheus-like at an Eurydice;
> For so delicious were the words she sung,
> It seem'd he had lov'd them a whole summer long.
> (I, 246-249)

The Orpheus-Eurydice image here is perfect, foreshadowing the tragedy that is to come, and to some extent identifying the flaw of Lycius with that of Orpheus. Orpheus, a mortal who cannot control his impatience, looks back a moment too soon, thus destroying himself and Eurydice; Lycius loses Lamia and his own life through a different mortal flaw, that of pride. Both Lycius and Orpheus contribute to their own destruction.

As the temptation progresses, Lycius, loving only the mere voice of the goddess, becomes completely entranced by her physical beauty:

> And soon his eyes had drunk her beauty up,
> Leaving no drop in the bewildering cup,
> And still the cup was full. (I, 251-253)

Strangely enough, he is almost immediately frightened that this vision will vanish. Lamia had told him to look back, to take her away from the lonely hills (the lone hills' side?). His reply repeatedly strikes the theme of disappearance, although she had given him as yet no indication that she had any intention of vanishing:

> Leave thee alone! Look back! Ah, Goddess, see
> Whether my eyes can ever turn from thee!
> For pity do not this sad heart belie –
> Even as thou vanishest so shall I die.
> Stay! though a Naiad of the rivers, stay!
> To thy far wishes will thy streams obey:
> Stay! though the greenest woods be thy domain,
> Alone they can drink up the morning rain:
> Though a descended Pleiad, will not one
> Of thine harmonious sisters keep in tune
> Thy spheres, and as thy silver proxy shine?
> So sweetly to these ravish'd ears of mine
> Came thy sweet greeting, that if thou should'st fade
> Thy memory will waste me to a shade:
> For pity, do not melt! (I, 275-289)

These lines contain four distinct references to the possibility of Lamia's disappearance; and Lycius thus indirectly prophesies not only his own death but also the tragic ending of the poem. But it is immediately made clear that simply by having appeared to him, by making herself known, she has become necessary to his continued existence. In a sense, there is really no temptation involved here; Lycius has no choice. Presumably the mere sound of her voice, her appearance to his mortal eyes, has left him no alternative but to succumb. If she should fade, the memory of her, like the memory of the poet's vision in Shelley's *Alastor,* will bring about his destruction.

As if to underscore her value to Lycius, Lamia now pretends that she must return to the purer realms. Capitalizing upon the suggestions of Lycius that she must be a goddess, some spirit from another world, she threatens to disappear:

> ". . . Alas! poor youth,
> What taste of purer air hast thou to soothe
> My essence?[23] What serener palaces,
> Where I may all my many senses please,
> And by mysterious sleights a hundred thirsts appease?
> It cannot be – Adieu!" (I, 281-286)

---

[23] *Essence* is used here, as in *Endymion,* to refer to a physical manifestation.

I suppose this threat of Lamia's to disappear could indicate that she is merely toying with Lycius, playing with him as a huntress might play with her prey. She knows the effect she has had on him and such an action might indicate a certain lack of compassion on her part. Such a reading is strengthened as the lines progress; Lycius has swooned, "pale with pain", as Lamia threatens to disappear:

> The cruel lady, without any show
> Of sorrow for her tender favourite's woe,
> But rather, if her eyes could brighter be,
> With brighter eyes and slow amenity,
> Put her new lips to his, and gave afresh
> The life she had so tangled in her mesh: (I, 290-295)

The word "cruel" here, the only time in the poem that it or any other such adjective is applied to Lamia, accompanied by her almost gloating absorption in her victim, her eyes gleaming at having him "so tangled in her mesh", does not create a particularly pleasant picture. However, in the complete context of the poem, the scene need not be interpreted as a sign that Lycius has succumbed to the charms of an "evil" temptress. Like a lady in a tale of courtly love, Lamia hides her true feelings, shows no outward indication of sorrow for the agony of her beseeching lover even though inwardly she is quite sympathetic to his feelings. In spite of her "cruelty", Lycius is still her "tender favourite"; as soon as she sees the extremity of pain to which her coyness has reduced him, she immediately restores him to hope and life.

The kiss with which she revives him is a rejuvenating kiss. Far from summoning up images of vampires sucking blood from their victims, or a temptress like Spenser's Acrasia sucking Verdant's manhood from his eyes as he sleeps, Lamia's action breathes new life into Lycius; she "puts her lips to his, and gave afresh/ The life she had so tangled in her mesh", just as Cynthia's kiss revives Endymion. Her action is the exact reverse of that of a vampire or evil enchantress. It is far closer to the action of God in *Paradise Lost*, breathing life into Adam. She breathes a new life into Lycius, and later, after she reassures him that she is a real woman with no more "subtle fluid in her veins than throbbing blood", we see this

life-giving power in all of its full resurrecting significance as
"Lycius from death awoke into amaze". She is a force of rejuvena-
tion, of restoration, of pleasure and delight:

> And every word she spake enticed him on
> To unperplex'd delight and pleasure known. (I, 326-327)

The short hymn of praise to the superiority of real women "lineal
indeed from Pyrrha's pebbles or Adam's seed" over supernatural
creatures such as "Faeries, Peris, Goddesses", which follows the
reawakening of Lycius is, of course, preparatory to Lamia's deci-
sion to "throw the Goddess off" and win her man by being merely
mortal. But these are important lines, suggesting as they do the
Endymion-Cynthia-Indian maiden relationship in Book Four of
Endymion. Cynthia wins the love of Endymion while in her role
of goddess, but she is unable to bring this love to full fruition until
she has also won him in her role as a creature of earth – the Indian
maiden.

The situation is paralleled in *Lamia*: Lamia wins the love of
Lycius while playing the role of goddess, and Lycius believes, at
first, that she is a goddess. But, like Cynthia, she

> ... threw the goddess off, and won his heart
> More pleasantly by playing woman's part,
> With no more awe than what her beauty gave,
> That while it smote, still guaranteed to save. (I, 336-339)

Lamia is not, as Wasserman claims, an unearthly version of
Cynthia; she is Cynthia with a new name. Her transformation
from goddess to woman has the same function in this poem as
Cynthia's disguise in *Endymion*. Here, as in the longer poem,
Keats is clearly making the point that the love which is ultimately
apotheosized is physical, earthly love, not ideal, or other-worldly.
"I was a woman once", Lamia explains to Hermes, and in spite of
her magical trappings, the ghostly palace in Corinth where "none
but feet divine could e'er have touched", rising in a space with no
physical dimensions, Lamia is a woman again. She uses no immortal charms or spells to enchant Lycius – she uses only her
physical, womanly beauty.

The first part of the poem closes on a note of ominous foreboding:

> And but the flitter-winged verse must tell
> For truth's sake, what woe afterwards befel,
> 'Twould humor many a heart to leave them thus
> Shut from the busy world of more incredulous. (I, 394-397)

But it also suggests the source of the woe to come: it will come from the "busy world". The evil is not to be found in the enchanted palace: Lycius has, upon entering this "purple-lined palace of sweet sin", reached the heights of love that Hermes had previously reached. He need not fade as mortals do; but he must be content to stay where he is – and the busy world must leave the lovers alone.

As the narrative continues, the two lovers are enthroned side by side in the palace, complete and self-sufficient in their immersion in each other:

> there they reposed
> Where use had made it sweet, with eyelids closed,
> Saving a tythe which love still open kept,
> That they might see each other while they almost slept.
> (II, 22-25)

Suddenly this scene of love's perfection is disturbed by the "thrill of trumpets", symbols of the outside world, much as Porphyro and Madeline are awakened by the "iced gusts" of the external world. This martial sound brings Lycius from his dream-sleep, making him aware of the "busy world" for the first time since his meeting with Lamia:

> His spirit pass'd beyond its golden bourn
> Into the noisy world almost forsworn. (I, 32-33)

Apparently all has gone well with the lovers until the outside world suddenly and intrusively breaks in upon them: but this blare of trumpets has an effect on Lycius that starts the sequence of tragic events leading to the final catastrophe. This intrusion and Lycius' reaction to it is responsible for everything that follows. Lamia is not responsible for it, and Apollonius is only one of the agents of the "noisy world". Lycius, being mortal, perhaps cannot avoid heeding the call of the anti-love forces in the outside world, as Wasserman believes; [24] but his insistence upon issuing from the palace to the outside world is certainly presented as a kind of weakness. In refusing to follow love, he destroys himself.

The relationship of Lycius and Lamia begins now to undergo a marked change. Whereas before Lamia has dominated the action, creating the palace, breathing life into Lycius, moving them through the streets of Corinth unseen, Lycius begins to assert himself as soon as he hears the trumpets. As though the sound had transformed him from his state of Hermes-like bliss, he begins to experience a worldly, earth-bound sense of pride in his accomplishments; in response to Lamia's obvious distress at his reaction to this recall to reality and her awareness that some part of him has deserted her, he replies that he is only concerned with

> . . . how to entangle, trammel up and snare
> Your soul in mine and labyrinth you there. (II, 52-53)

All previous images in the poem of entanglement, snaring, and trapping, had been in connection with Lamia's effect upon Lycius; but now he wishes to assert his dominance – from the entangled he wishes to become the entangler. He proposes to take his bride before the world, to show her off before the "rude" Corinthians.

> What mortal hath a prize, that other men
> May be confounded and abash'd withal,
> But lets it sometimes pace abroad majestical,
> And triumph, as in thee I should rejoice
> Amid the hoarse alarm of Corinth's voice.
> Let my foes choke, and my friends shout afar,
> While through the thronged streets your bridal car
> Wheels round its dazzling spokes. (II, 57-64)

Lycius in thus asserting himself reveals a grossness of motive: he wishes to "let his foes choke", to bring Lamia home in triumph, to hear the thunderous applause of the world. He misses the point that Lamia and his present state of bliss are only possible when the world's motives and petty problems are inoperative. And when Lamia, knowing what the result of this world's madness will be, resists him, Lycius asserts his worldly, masculine dominance over her for the first time:

> He . . . was stung,
> Perverse, with stronger fancy to reclaim
> Her wild and timid nature to his aim:
> Besides, for all his love, in self despite
> Against his better self, he took delight
> Luxurious in her sorrows, soft and new.
> His passion, cruel grown, took on a hue
> Fierce and sanguineous as 'twas possible
> In one whose brow had no dark veins to swell.
> Fine was the mitigated fury, like
> Apollo's presence when in act to strike
> The serpent. (II, 69-80)

Lamia, having previously thrown off the goddess, now must play the part of the traditional submissive female of the dominant male; she gives in with no strong protest, even though aware of what this submissiveness will mean:

> . . . She burnt, she lov'd the tyranny,
> And, all subdued, consented to the hour
> When to the bridal he should lead the paramour.
> (II, 82-84)

Lamia is no longer the goddess of love, dominating the action. She submits to the masculine tyranny, and the die is cast. Henceforth the only concession Lycius makes to Lamia's wishes is to refuse to invite Apollonius to the wedding feast – a last attempt to delay the inevitable.

For Apollonius, the symbol of reason and the enquiring mind, the publicly motivated and responsible element in man's make-up, must by the very nature of these things he symbolically represents, destroy Lamia and the pleasure palace. It doesn't matter if he is invited to the feast; once Lamia and her golden palace are exposed to the world's eyes, the Apolloniuses of the world must examine, probe, and "murder to dissect".

The tragic conclusion of the poem is therefore inevitable, once Lycius determines to assert this masculine dominance. This assertion of self – the mortal, conscious, egotistical self – over the dream

assures his own destruction. Once the love-world is gone, once the
dream is destroyed, Lycius is dead. The sterile, reasonable world
dominated by Apollonius and his piercing intellect is not enough.
Man cannot live when philosophy has destroyed the main impetus
for living:

> Do not all charms fly
> At the mere touch of cold philosophy?
> There was an awful rainbow once in heaven:
> We know her woof, her texture; she is given
> In the dull catalogue of common things.
> Philosophy will clip an Angel's wings,
> Conquer all mysteries by rule and line,
> Empty the haunted air, and gnomed mine –
> Unweave a rainbow, as it erewhile made
> The tender-person'd Lamia melt into a shade.
>
> (II, 229-238)

As Apollonius confronts Lamia in the banquet hall, there is little
doubt that Keats meant the victory of Apollonius to be seen as a
hollow one. The sage destroys Lamia with a merciless and dedicated precision. As Lycius sees her withering under the old man's
gaze, he curses the old man:

> "Shut, shut those juggling eyes, thou ruthless man!
> Turn them aside, wretch! or the righteous ban
> Of all the Gods . . .
> May pierce them on the sudden with the thorn
> Of painful blindness." (II, 278-282)

The old man's exorcism of the tender-personed Lamia is offensive
to the gods; rather than saving, he is destroying. His philosophy
and presumably rationalistic teachings are called "impious, proud-
heart sophistries", "unlawful magic", "enticing lies". Lycius denounces the philosopher in precisely the same terms that the
philosopher would use to denounce the enchantress: to the rational,
ordered intellect, Lamia would be the "impious" one; she would
be the author of "enticing lies" or the practitioner of "unlawful
magic".

Lycius calls the attention of the assembly to the old man's intense, almost frenzied manner:

Corinthians! look upon that grey-beard wretch!
Mark how, possessed, his lashless eyelids stretch
Around his demon eyes! (II, 287-289)

The destroyer of demons is described in demonic terms. The old
man is the one possessed – the lashless eyelids suggest, of all
things, a serpent! The eyes are demon eyes, cruel, avenging, and
contemptuous.

Relentlessly the old man continues his ungodly work, answering
the pleas of Lycius to stop with contemptuous scorn:

"Fool! Fool! . . .
. . . from every ill
Of life have I preserved thee to this day,
And shall I see thee made a serpent's prey?" (II, 295-298)

At the sound of the word "serpent", Lamia "breathed deep
breath", and with her weak hand "motioned him to be silent" as
if the sophist's word is perhaps more potent than his eye. But
Apollonius, "look'd and look'd again", repeating the word like a
magic spell.

"A serpent!" cried he; no sooner said
Than with a frightful scream she vanished. (II, 305-306)

The combination of the word and the look have destroyed; Lamia,
named as serpent, now is serpent. She has probably returned to
the immortal world, to her "wreathed tomb". As the knights and
warriors identify the lady of the meads as La Belle Dame Sans
Merci, so Apollonius identifies the beautiful Lamia as serpent.
Once the act of naming takes place, the thing becomes the thing
so named. Naming her evil makes her evil, or at least her effect
upon her lover becomes evil. Like the knight-at-arms, Lycius is
destroyed when the world insists that devotion to the erotic is evil.

. . . Lycius' arms were empty of delight
As were his limbs of life, from that same night.

Delight and life are thus identified; the possession of Lamia had
been life – she had breathed life into him, revived his fallen spirit,
made him whole. Her destruction is death; when the bride is
destroyed, Lycius marries death. The last line prepares us for this

grim marriage as the "heavy body" is wound "in its marriage robe", contrasting vividly with his marriage to Lamia.

Lamia then, like *La Belle Dame,* is not a poem in which erotic love is denounced or even dismissed. In fact, such love is once more defined as the supreme value, the destruction of which leads to death. But in both poems, the possibility of love's fulfillment in the corrupt world of man is no longer certain. The forces of this world, moral, religious, and social, which in *Endymion* and *The Eve of St. Agnes* could be defeated, are now triumphant. But the triumph, although perhaps inevitable under existing circumstances, is shallow and hollow. The world may win, but the price of victory is death of the spirit. Man without the "elfin grot" or the "pleasure palace" is left like the dying knight-at-arms "on the cold hillside", "alone and palely loitering", or like Lycius, bereft of life itself.

EROS AND THE ROMANTICS

In the preceding studies we have seen an attitude toward the erotic representing a sharp shift from the orthodox Christian ethos. Coleridge, Shelley, and Keats describe the universe in human rather than superhuman terms: their values are centered in man. The divine is worthy of worship only in so far as it reflects, realistically and accurately, that which is in man. The deity is no abstract, absolute, and arbitrary figure, imposing his decrees upon humanity, decrees that contradict the basic nature of man. The gods have become internalized; they reside in the human psyche, and their external manifestations are but reflections of what is internal.

Thus questions of good and evil become something far more complex than the traditional, Christian dichotomy which sees God as good, but a good approachable only if man puts down the brute aspects of his nature, those aspects which are antithetical to the divine. Although Christ may have said that the kingdom of God is within, he did not suggest by this that God himself existed primarily as an internal force. Traditional Christianity depends for its validity upon a belief, on the metaphysical plane, in a hierarchical system of which man is a part, and on the moral plane, a belief in a hierarchical system of values against which man may measure his actions. The Romantics are not totally without a system of values; indeed much of their efforts may be defined as a search for a system of values to replace one which had decayed. But their system of values is in many areas, particularly in the area of the erotic passions, markedly different from the traditional.

The key idea in the Romantic concept of the struggle between the warring elements in man's nature is one of *reconciliation* rather than *opposition*. Instead of opposing "sense" to "spirit", or "body" to "soul", the Romantics seem to be trying to heal the tortured human psyche. They are not even Manicheans finding meaning in the perpetual conflict between equally powerful forces, although their attempts to redefine the elements in the cosmic struggle may resemble the Manichean idea at times. They no longer define spirituality as *good*, sensuality as *bad* or *less good*; and, like the Manicheans, they feel that spirit and sense are inextricably interwoven in man's nature. But they do not accept the necessity of eternal struggle; the Romantics are seeking the kind of integration of the psyche to which Freud and Jung will later give their names.

Each poet attacks the problem differently, but a common bond unites all three: a realization that the orthodox, static, fixed, mechanistic universe is inadequate. All three attempt to discover a new cosmic metaphor to define man's position.

Coleridge, as we have seen, is perhaps not fully conscious of what he is doing. But his very lack of public awareness has made his efforts symbolically more interesting. Without a fixed, conscious attempt to redefine his moral universe, but with an indefinitive sense that all was not well with the old view, his splendid and fragmentary poems reveal the difficulty of pinning down this new vision with complete accuracy.

In both *Kubla Khan* and *Christabel*, we see the poet struggling to redefine the nature of the psychic struggle, to discover some metaphor or image which will more accurately describe it. He realizes that the old "pleasure garden" of well-ordered, rationalistic thought is inadequate. Forces exist that must by their very nature threaten this geometric Paradise when such a Paradise is imposed or decreed. The sacred river cannot be dammed; the romantic chasm cannot be ignored or, worse yet, relegated to an inferior position. It will burst through and destroy whatever tries to limit or compress it. And Geraldine cannot be kept from the castle; Christabel, in spite of her piety, her innocence, her faith, must be seduced. And if the education of Christabel means the destruction of the castle and the well-ordered but life-in-death atmosphere which permeates it, then so it must be. Geraldine triumphs, not because evil triumphs over good in a distorted Christian vision; she triumphs because of a necessitarian principle. If man is to live as a whole rather than as a divided creature, then what has been thought of as evil must be described and evaluated in some other terms. These terms may not be pleasant; perhaps the entire process of awakening may be painful; but the forces of Eros must prevail. Suppression of them means a death-like sleep for man – a sleep in which he is unaware of his affinity with earth and nature.

That the erotic impulse, the sexual principle, as represented by both the sacred river and Geraldine has been traditionally associated with something baleful and malevolent, especially when rigidly and tightly controlled and regulated, is irrelevant. In a human-oriented universe we must make do with what is human, with *all* that is human, even that which is unpleasant.

Coleridge's attitude toward this new awareness is, of course, ambiguous, particularly when such awareness involves the erotic. His attempt to act in such a way as to cast no aspersions on his character in his extremely unhappy marriage, his behavior toward Sara Hutchinson with whom he was deeply and passionately in love, his complete religious orthodoxy in his later life, all suggest that whatever private insight or awareness he possessed was expressed only in his verse, and even there, ambiguously and symbolically. Never, as in the case of Shelley, did he discuss or analyze his speculations on the nature of the erotic publicly. Certainly he was a man torn between an orthodox, public, and social moral code and a private suspicion that such a code was inadequate and perhaps destructive.

Shelley presents a totally different case. Not only does his poetry frankly and enthusiastically endorse a commitment to erotic love as a means of breaking through to something which ultimately transcends the physical experience; he acted on this principle in his own private affairs. His continual refusal to confine his own erotic feelings to one person is well known, perhaps too well known. For too often the casual reader is more interested in the "amorous" Shelley of legend than the "poetic" Shelley who attempted to create in his verse a fairly coherent philosophical and moral system based upon "sweet, human love".

Shelley's poetry, as opposed to Coleridge's, is not in the least ambiguous when examined closely. And his attitudes toward the erotic are similarly obvious. Shelley makes it abundantly clear that the old moral order is inadequate as a means of handling the forces of Eros. His attack in *Alastor* on a total commitment to abstract and philosophical thought at the expense of human involvement reveals the inadequacy of rationalistic thought as a primary value. Although he does not, as Keats does in *Lamia*, see the philosophical quest as a destroyer in itself, he nonetheless attempts to question the value of such a quest.

Epipsychidion is a frank celebration of erotic love as a means of achieving a mystic union with the ideal. Here Shelley, much as Keats does in *Endymion*, explores the process by which the ideal and the divine can be realized in human terms. The beautiful vision becomes beautiful woman. By moving from human society with its vulgarization of the erotic, its attempts to control and denigrate the erotic spirit in the iron bands of monogamy, to an erotic Paradise, the poet-narrator of *Epipsychidion* humanizes the ideal without corrupting it. The ideal is impossible and unattainable unless it is firmly based upon the human. In Shelley we have the most conscious and deliberate attempt to heal, to integrate the warring elements in man's psyche. Although he may oversimplify, dismissing the enormous power of the social world to entangle man, making man psychologically incapable of the total isolation from it Shelley prescribes, he is nonetheless laying down a kind of formula for personal salvation through devotion to Eros. These are the terms of reconciliation, Shelley seems to be saying; by these means we may satisfy the demands of the spirit without dismissing, ignoring, or destroying our physical being.

If Coleridge recognizes, however ambiguously, the symptoms of the decaying moral order in its unalterable conflict, and to some extent can isolate some of the reasons for its decay, and Shelley prescribes a limited but fairly coherent remedy, in Keats we have the most profound awareness of the difficulties that lie in the way of a reconciliation. In the early poems, *Endymion* and *The Eve* of *St. Agnes*, Keats shared Shelley's belief that dedication to the senses was the way to salvation. Actually he takes this idea a step further. Whereas Shelley sees sensual love as the basis for approaching the ideal, Keats, especially in *Endymion* and *St. Agnes*, deifies the sensual, replacing the old gods with the triumphant forces of Eros.

But in his last two poems, as we have seen, without deviating from his conviction that the erotic may well be man's salvation, he realizes the combination of social and psychological pressures that resist such dedication on the mortal level. Man may well have learned what the key to salvation is, but he is not yet ready to use it. The elfin grot and the pleasure palace have been located (they are symbolically the same as Shelley's Aegean isle). But Keats realizes that not only is the journey hazardous, the effort required to break with the mainland is almost superhuman. And the blare of trumpets from the world travels a long way; its "silver snarl" is apparently as irresistible as the siren's call.

The siren-Odysseus metaphor suggests clearly an interesting reversal of the traditional moral order in Keats. Instead of Odysseus in his boat, traveling past the sensuous maidens, and saved from destruction only because he is tied to the mast, the image suggested by Keats is that of Odysseus among the sirens. The treacherous voice is coming from the ship, trying to bring him back to the world. And because both the knight-at-arms in *La Belle Dame* and Lycius in *Lamia* heed the call of the "noisy world, almost forsworn", they are destroyed.

The implications of this Romantic vision to the student of literature are enormous. If one thinks about it for a moment, he begins to realize that this revolt from the traditional God-centered universe toward a cosmic metaphor centered around man is a movement that continues in modern literature. Lawrence, Yeats, and the early Eliot are obvious literary heirs of the Romantics; their works are explorations of and elaborations upon the themes opened by the pioneering of the Romantics. *The Wasteland* has been called a great Romantic poem: more than that, it is a great Romantic poem on precisely the same theme we have encountered throughout the study – the possibility of spiritual salvation through

sexual regeneration. Eliot's portrait of a society spiritually desic-
cated is presented throughout in sexual metaphors. The drawing
room society of Prufrock, capsulized in the boudoir scene of the
second part of *The Wasteland*, is a spiritually empty world – and
the emptiness is not a result, at least here, of man's falling away
from God, but of man's falling away from man, or better yet,
falling away from woman. The neurotic female and her impotent
companion, too well-bred to acknowledge the source of their
frustrations, wait in love-less, sex-less, ennui for the knock upon
the door. And the scene in the pub, immediately following, develops the theme of the vulgarity to which the sex act can be brought,
the triviality that it assumes in human life when the source of life
and creativity becomes mechanical and cheap. In the pub scene,
the primary consideration in the cheap talk of sex and contra-
ceptives is how life can be aborted.

Throughout *The Wasteland* the interrelatedness of sexuality and
spirituality is examined. The world waits, perhaps hopelessly, for
the deliverer, the new messiah, the modern Galahad whose
spiritual purity has nothing to do with chastity and whose primary
function will be to heal through a spiritual regeneration of sex.
Only when sex has been placed on a level where it can dignify and
create, will the world be cured of its spiritual dry-rot.

Yeats is similarly concerned with the effect upon man's spirit
and imagination of sexual impotency. Throughout *The Tower*
runs the theme of the close relation of sexuality to creativity. The
old man wonders if this "absurdity", this "caricature" of a body
hung upon his spirit by "decrepit age" will dry up the source of
his poetry. Having outlived the sexual impulses, he sees himself a
"battered kettle" tied to a dog's tail, no longer able to tap the
sources of poetry at their roots in the sexual. Nothing is left
him but abstract and philosophical speculation: his imagination
must "be content with argument and deal/ In abstract things".
('It seems that I must bid the Muse go pack,/ Choose Plato
and Plotinus for a friend.") He resolves at the end of the
poem to compose his soul in the face of this, to compel it to
study

> In a learned school
> Till the wreck of body,
> Slow decay of blood,
> Testy delirium
> Or dull decrepitude,
> Or what worse evils come.

But such resolution, like his resolution in *Sailing to Byzantium*, to leave the sensual world for the monuments of unaging intellect", is no rejection of sexuality as such. Yeats makes it clear that "That is no country for old men". The implication is that it *is* the country for young men; and for young men prepared to commit themselves to their own proud flesh, the poet passes on his holy robes:

> I leave both faith and pride
> To young upstanding men
> Climbing the mountain-side,
> That under bursting dawn
> They may drop a fly;
> Being of that metal made
> Till it was broken by
> This sedentary trade.

Impotency is equated with abstraction and death, sexuality with the world of the senses and life. Byzantium may be an escape from the sensual world; but there is little suggestion that the sensual world with "the young in one another's arms" is a dangerous delusion, something to be avoided. It is the world in which man spends the greater part of his life. And even more, it is the source of even "the monuments of unaging intellect", poetry and the arts. Once we have left, we must, like the aging poet in the tower, "bid the Muse go pack".

Finally, in D. H. Lawrence we find the sexual and erotic specifically and non-symbolically identified with mystic fulfillment. Lawrence's ethos, a complete dedication to the sexual, insists upon the elimination of any restraint upon the free expression of sexual feeling. As Lady Chatterly is revived from her spiritual death-bed by the earth-centered gardener, so is Paul Morel nearly destroyed by the sexual puritan who is his mother. The forces of Eros when allowed free expression revive and purify; when restrained and contaminated by societal forces, the family, class distinctions, or the ossified intellect, Eros becomes a destroyer instead of the deliverer.

In short, then, it is time to start reading the Romantic poets as the pioneers of our own age, rather than trying to fit them into the context of an era with which they are trying to break. The Romantic revolt may be one of the most significant movements in human history; the poets and writers of the movement are involved in a struggle almost unprecedented. Although the Renaissance is generally considered the fore-runner of our modern civilization, it should be realized that the job of the Renaissance poet was of far less proportions than that of the Romantic. For the Renaissance is trying to re-examine the relations between God and man but in the context of the same cosmic scheme that had prevailed from antiquity. So far as we know there was little attempt among the English Renaissance writers to move God out of his heaven and establish him entirely in the human psyche. He still reigned supreme, even though humanity and the earth regained some importance in the cosmic scheme. But Milton's God is an authoritarian God, an absolute God, who rules and decrees and punishes for disobedience. The Romantic God is created by a kind of dialectic; if spirit and sense can become fused into one indivisible harmonious whole, the psychic struggle may be resolved. Evil is not the result of man's fall from a previous state of grace: evil is the result of man's failure to unite the warring elements, one of which had been traditionally identified with the cause of evil.

Such a departure from the orthodox conception represents, it seems to me, far more than a modification of the role of God in order to establish the possibility of human dignity. In fact, the Romantic revolt is not a modification at all: it is a complete and startling revolution in man's thinking, throwing away all of the old and established forms of belief and involving what amounts to a start from the beginning. The revolution is still in process; and the modern world often seems a wilderness, now that the easy to read signposts have been destroyed. Pain and horror and ugliness surround us as the apparent result of our departure from the *ancien regime*. And looking back we may even long for the moral security offered by the world we have left.

Many of us can cross the centuries and read Donne, for instance, as pertinent to our age, but in many cases we fail to be sympathetic to much Romantic poetry. We mistakenly regard some of the Romantics as perverted offshoots of the old tradition or as highly refined young men talking in highly abstract symbols. However, they are not bright but ineffectual angels; they are men concerned with the *human* nature of man. We read them wrong and do ourselves a disservice if we fail to see that they are part of our own world dealing with the very real problems and conflicts with which we are still faced.

LIST OF WORKS CITED

Akenside, Mark, "The Pleasure of Imagination", *The Works of the English Poets*, ed. Alexander Chalmers (n.p., 1810), 60-80.

Angus, Douglas, "The Theme of Love and Guilt in Coleridge's Three Major Poems", *JEGP*, LIX (1960), 655-668.

Baker, Carlos H., *Shelley's Major Poetry: The Fabric of a Vision* (Princeton, Princeton University Press, 1948).

Barnard, Ellsworth, *Shelley's Religion* (Minneapolis, University of Minnesota Press, 1936).

Basler, Roy P., *Sex, Symbolism and Psychology in Literature* (New Brunswick, Rutgers University Press, 1948).

Blackstone, Bernard, *The Consecrated Urn* (London, Longman's Green, 1959).

Bostetter, Edward E., "*Christabel:* The Vision of Fear", *PQ*, XXXVI (1957), 183-194.

——, "Shelley and the Mutinous Flesh", *Texas Studies in Language and Literature*, I (1959), 203-213.

Campbell, Olwen W., *Shelley and the Unromantics* (London, Methuen and Co., Ltd., 1924).

Clapp, Edwin R., "La Belle Dame as Vampire", *PQ*, XXVII (1948), 89-92.

Coleridge, Samuel Taylor, *The Poems of Coleridge* (London, Oxford University Press, 1960).

Colvin, Sidney, *John Keats* (New York, Charles Scribners and Sons, 1925).

DeSelincourt, Ernest, *Oxford Lectures on Poetry* (Oxford, Clarendon Press, 1934).

——, ed., *The Poems of John Keats*, 6th ed. (New York, Dodd Mead and Co., 1921).

Fausset, Hugh I'Anson, *Keats: A Study in Development* (London, M. Secker, 1922).

Finney, Claude, *The Evolution of Keats's Poetry* (Cambridge, Harvard University Press, 1936).

Foakes, R. A., *The Romantic Assertion* (New Haven, Yale University Press, 1958).

Fogle, Richard H., "The Romantic Unity of *Kubla Khan*", *College English*, XXII (1960), 112-116.

Ford, Newell F., "*Endymion:* A Neo-Platonic Allegory", *ELH*, XIV (1947), 64-78.

——, "The Meaning of 'Fellowship with Essence' in *Endymion*", *PMLA*, LXII (1947), 1061-1076.

——, *The Prefigurative Imagination of John Keats* (Stanford, Stanford University Press, 1951).

Garrod, H. W., *Keats* (Oxford, Clarendon Press, 1926).

Gibson, Evan K., "*Alastor:* A Reinterpretation", *PMLA*, LXII (1947), 1022-1045.

Grabo, Carl H., *The Magic Plant: The Growth of Shelley's Thought* (Chapel Hill, Duke University Press, 1936).

Graves, Robert, *The Meaning of Dreams* (London, Adelphi Company, 1924).

Havens, R. D., "Shelley's *Alastor*", *PMLA*, XLV (1930), 1098-1115.

Heninger, S. K., J., "A Jungian Reading of *Kubla Khan*", *JAAC*, XVIII (1960), 358-367.

Hoffman, Harold L., *An Odyssey of the Soul: Shelley's "Alastor"* (New York, Columbia University Press, 1933).

Keats, John, *The Poems of John Keats* (London, Oxford University Press, 1960).

Lovejoy, Arthur O., *The Great Chain of Being* (Cambridge, Harvard University Press, 1936).

Lowes, John Livingston, *The Road to Xanadu* (New York, Houghton Mifflin, 1927).

Knight, G. Wilson, *The Starlit Dome* (London, Oxford University Press, 1941).

Murry, John Middleton, *Keats* (New York, Noonday Press, 1955).

——, *Keats and Shakespeare* (London, Oxford University Press, 1925).

——, *Studies in Keats, New and Old* (London, Oxford University Press, 1939).

Nethercot, Arthur H., *The Road to Tryermaine* (Chicago, University of Chicago Press, 1939).

Notopoulos, James A., *The Platonism of Shelley* (Durham, Duke University Press, 1949).

Owens, F. W., *John Keats: A Study* (London, Kegan Paul and Co., 1880).

Peckham, Morse, "Toward a Theory of Romanticism", *PMLA*, LXVI (1951), 5-23.

Pettet, E. C., *On the Poetry of Keats* (Cambridge, Cambridge University Press, 1957).

Potter, Stephen, *Coleridge and S. T. C.* (Toronto, Thomas Nelson and Sons, 1935).

Schneider, Elizabeth, *Coleridge, Opium and "Kubla Khan"* (Chicago, University of Chicago Press, 1953).

Shelley, Percy Bysshe, *Shelley's Prose: The Trumpet of a Prophecy*, ed. David L. Clark (Alburquerque, University of New Mexico Press, 1954).

——, *The Poems of Shelley* (London, Oxford University Press, 1960).

Stallknecht, Newton P., *Strange Seas of Thought* (Bloomington, Indiana University Press, 1955).

——, "Wordsworth and the Quality of Man", *The Major English Romantic Poets* (Carbondale, Southern Illinois University Press, 1957).

Stoll, E. E., "Symbolism in Coleridge", *PMLA*, LXIII (1948), 214-233.

Stovall, Floyd, *Desire and Restraint in Shelley* (Durham, Duke University Press, 1931).

Suther, Marshall, "On the Interpretation of *Kubla Khan*", *Bucknell Review*, VII (1957), 1-19.

Thorpe, Clarence D., *The Mind of John Keats* (New York, Oxford University Press, 1926).

Utley, Francis L., "La Belle Dame and the Inferno of Lucretius", *ELH*, XXV (1958), 105-121.

Warren, Robert Penn, "A Poem of Pure Imagination", preface to *Rime of The Ancient Mariner* (New York, Reynal Publishing Co., 1946).

Warton, Joseph, "The Enthusiast", in *English Poems from Dryden to Blake*, ed. James W. Tupper (New York, Prentice-Hall, 1933).

Wasserman, Earl, *The Finer Tone* (Baltimore, Johns Hopkins Press, 1953).

White, Newman I., *Shelley*, 2 vols. (New York, A. A. Knopf, 1940).

Woodberry, George E., ed., *The Complete Poetical Works of Percy Bysshe Shelley* (Boston, Houghton, Mifflin and Co., 1901).

Wordsworth, William, *The Poetical Works of Wordsworth*, Oxford edition (London, Oxford University Press, 1960).

INDEX

STUDIES IN ENGLISH LITERATURE

16. BARBARA BARTHOLOMEW: *Fortuna and Natura: A Reading of Three Chaucer Narratives.* 1966. 112 pp. Cloth.   Gld. 17.—

17. GEORG B. FERGUSON: *John Fletcher: The Woman's Prize or The Tamer Tamed. A Critical Edition.* 1966. 223 pp. Cloth.
Gld. 24.—

18. EDWARD VASTA: *The Spiritual Basis of "Piers Plowman".* 1965. 143 pp. Cloth.   Gld. 18.—

19. WILLIAM B. TOOLE: *Shakespeare's Problem Plays: Studies in Form and Meaning.* 1966. 242 pp. Cloth.   Gld. 28.—

20. LOUISE BAUGHMAN MURDY: *Sound and Meaning in Dylan Thomas's Poetry.* 1966. 172 pp., 11 spectograms. Cloth.
Gld. 21.—

21. BEN H. SMITH: *Traditional Imagery of Charity in "Piers Plowman".* 1966. 106 pp. Cloth.   Gld. 14.—

22. OVERTON P. JAMES: *The Relation of Tristram Shandy to the Life of Sterne.* 1966. 174 pp. Cloth.   Gld. 21.—

23. LOUIS TONKO MILIC: *A Quantitative Approach to the Style of Jonathan Swift.* 1967. 317 pp., 56 tables, 15 figs., folding Key.
Gld. 34.—

25. BRADFORD B. BROUGHTON: *The Legends of King Richard I: Coeur de Lion: A Study of Sources and Variations to the Year 1600.* 1966. 161 pp. Cloth.   Gld. 20.—

26. WILLIAM M. WYNKOOP: *Three Children of the Universe: Emerson's View of Shakespeare, Bacon, and Milton.* 1966. 199 pp., portrait. Cloth.   Gld. 22.—

28. SOPHIA BLAYDES: *Christopher Smart as a Poet of His Time: A Re-Appraisal.* 1966. 182 pp. Cloth.   Gld. 24.—

29. ROBERT R. HODGES: *The Dual Heritage of Joseph Conrad.* 1967. 229 pp.   Gld. 27.—

30. GEORGE R. LEVINE: *Henry Fielding and the Dry Mock: A Study of the Techniques of Irony in His Early Works.* 1967. 160 pp.
Gld. 20.—

31. ERIC LAGUARDIA: *Nature Redeemed: The Imitation of Order in Three Renaissance Poems.* 1966. 180 pp. Cloth.   Gld. 20.—

34. ROBERT DONALD SPECTOR: *English Literary Periodicals and the Climate of Opinion during the Seven Years' War.* 1966. 408 pp.
Gld. 40.—

MOUTON — PUBLISHERS — THE HAGUE

DA⁻